NEVER BEYOND HOPE

How selfish lusts devastate families,
and how God redeems them.

DANIEL P. DOMBERG

Scripture quotations taken from The Holy Bible, New International Version® NIV®
Copyright © 1973 1978 1984 2011 by Biblica, Inc. TM
Used by permission. All rights reserved worldwide.

Published by Northeast Christian Resources
Foreword by Wayne Hume
Edited by Megan Ryan
Cover and Interior Design by Tanner DiGiovanni
Cover Images Courtesy of Lake City Reporter
Copyright © 2019 Daniel P. Domberg
All rights reserved.
ISBN 9781732720220:

TABLE OF CONTENTS

Foreword	5
Peace Through Pain	7
A Yearning	12
Wrong Turn	21
Out of Hand	32
Too Big For His Britches	41
The Void	52
Acting Out	59
Losing Faith	70
Adapting	74
The New Normal	82
Surrogates	90
Regret	98
Enough is Enough	103
The Way Of The Fool	110
Epiphany	117
The Trap	126
The War Within	131
Reunited	139
The Call	146
Revelation	153
Afterword	158

FOREWORD

When life begins, everything seems so simple—our point of reference, what brings joy, what brings sorrow, our diets, the people in our life. It is all so simple. Yet for each of us, there is a point in life when things become more complicated. The simple story we thought we were living has so many more wrinkles, facets, deep emotions, and moving parts. It can be really overwhelming when we finally recognize all the pieces that make up our story.

This is a look into one man's journey. It is a frank telling that artfully moves from a naïve childish perspective to painful but more mature understanding. The story speaks to identity lost, then identity found. It is transparent in the grief, the failing and the struggle it conveys.

In this story you will find parallels to your own. The names and events may be different, but the pain, the insecurities, the struggles will be the same. We all have these parts of our story. Some of us readily admit they exist. Some of us blame them for the choices we make. Some stuff them deep inside hoping to never see or feel them again. But we all have them.

I hope you don't miss the best part of this story. Beauty comes from ashes. Through Christ we can overcome all that could destroy us. Family history, dysfunctional environments, the destructive influence of those we look up to, and the temptation to seek escape and happiness in something or someone other than God's plan for us; all of these war against us and at times overcome us, but they do not have to destroy us. These negative experiences do not have to control the narrative, set our course, or enslave us. All of the ugly things from our past can become beautiful. We can overcome them! That is the divine mystery that is God's unfolding story that emerges within our own. Our ugly, broken, and embarrassing story is redeemed within God's gracious, merciful and good story.

Listen to Paul in 2 Corinthians 5:17-19, giving encouragement to people who had some pretty wicked and broken histories:

> "Therefore, if anyone is in Christ, the new creation has come: The old has gone, the new is here! All this is from God, who reconciled us to himself through Christ and gave us the ministry of reconciliation: that God was reconciling the world to himself in Christ, not counting people's sins against them. And he has committed to us the message of reconciliation."

Through Jesus we have the opportunity to write a very different ending to our stories. Instead of all of that pain and struggling destroying all that is good in our life, God restores us in His eyes and we get the chance to help others be restored as well.

In the telling of this story, Dan is doing exactly that. He is conveying his own restoration and reconciliation and in telling the story, he is conveying the hope of restoration to each of us.

Do not miss the opportunity to hear this story, to see yourself in it, and accept the offer to be restored as well.

Wayne Hume
Lead Pastor
Northeast Christian Church
Rockford, IL

Chapter One

PEACE THROUGH PAIN

August 4th, 2009

John 16:33 – I have told you these things, so that in me you may have peace. In this world you will have trouble. But take heart! I have overcome the world.

He almost dropped his cell phone when she told him.

This day started off like any other Tuesday for Danny. He woke up, ate breakfast, showered, kissed Julie, hugged his kids and headed off to work. It was a fairly slow day in the office. The meeting schedule was light; there were no quality crises to contend with. He was busying himself with some mundane task in the late morning when the call came in.

He paused when he saw the caller ID. *Why would Aunt Sandy be calling me now*? he wondered. He deliberated for a few seconds, his thumb hovering over the "send to voicemail" icon. But he knew this could be something bad. Maybe Grandma Alice was in the hospital? Maybe Aunt Debbie was in an accident? Or maybe…

"Hey Aunt Sandy," he greeted, trying to sound light and optimistic.

"Hello Danny, is this a good time to talk?" Sandy always had a droning cadence to her voice, but she sounded particularly weary and sad.

"Yeah, I'm not too busy right now."

"Well, unfortunately, I have to let you know that your dad passed away yesterday."

Those words echoed in his mind as she continued talking. His head fell, and the beige cubicle walls enclosing him felt like they were squeezing in around him. He didn't really pay attention to what she said after that. Instead, his mind flashed to when they'd go and feed the ducks at the local pond and to all the boring Blackhawks games. Then to his memory of the last time he saw him, four years ago. He couldn't believe that that would be the last time.

In reality, this news wasn't such a big of a surprise to Danny. Or at least it shouldn't have been. His dad's health had been deteriorating for years. His history of heart disease combined with the stress and poor diet of incarceration didn't give him good prospects for a long life. He had been moved around the past several months from one medical facility to another as he contended with a myriad of ailments. His Grandma Alice couldn't keep track of his location, and she was more frustrated and worried than usual with her inability to locate him or get a status on his condition. She debated flying to Florida herself or hiring a private investigator, but she didn't have the energy or financial wherewithal after twenty-seven years of fighting for her oldest son. So Danny had been praying about this for a while. And he had been mentally preparing himself for the worst. So that's what shocked him most of all about hearing the news. He wasn't reacting as he thought he would.

He tried to plow through his workday, but the lack of anything pressing allowed his mind and heart to wander. He would start to type out an email and find himself staring blankly at the screen. He felt an overwhelming need to get out of there, to run away somehow. He tried walking around the building, but the feelings returned once he stopped moving. Finally, he sent his boss an email and told him the news. He didn't ask if he could take the rest of the day off. He told him he needed to, and he left.

During the dull ride home, his thoughts and emotions intertwined in a tempest of unrest. Sports radio didn't soothe or distract; he paid it no mind. There was nothing about the passing farmlands to pique his interest or get his attention. He was focused on this feeling he'd never really experienced before. Hope was dead.

When he got home, Julie's face reflected Danny's feelings. "You need to go for a run or something, clear your mind," she suggested.

Danny wore his bravest face and nodded. He changed into running clothes, laced up his shoes, queued up his music and headed out on the course he had run so many times before. But this was the only one he would ever truly remember.

The humid August air of northern Illinois felt good that day. The sun was shining and the leaves danced as he ran down the road from his house. The smell of fresh-cut grass brought to mind an early memory of his dad cutting the grass back in Palos.

The music in his ears played like a perfect soundtrack as his mind bubbled with memories, fleeting and random: sitting at the big desk at the auto-parts store, stamping documents his dad gave him as busy work. The long drives to downtown Chicago twice a week for the couple of years he was housed there. The time he got a spanking with the belt for lying about hurting his brother. The guns. The lottery tickets. That last visit.

But even more than that, his heart felt the knot of what would never be. As his feet pounded with each step, the knot grew larger and larger. From the time he was first told about his dad being in jail, when he was nine years old, he always fantasized about seeing him free again. At first, the fantasies would be about how he would swoop back in and rescue the struggling auto-parts store or maybe get remarried to his mom. When the reality of his dad's sentence and improbable release came to mind, it was about what it would be like to live in prison with him. Danny knew his power and influence didn't end when he went to prison; it just changed. He imagined living his days in the cold, structured regime, making the most of it as his dad's apprentice.

In the last few years, the daydreams surrounded what it would be like to see Dad get out of prison now that Danny had achieved some success of his own. How he could help him get back on his feet, maybe help get him a job. How they'd get a case of beer or a bottle of whiskey and just play cards one night and get brutally honest about what really happened. After struggling through this for twenty-seven years himself, Danny had a pretty good idea of what went down. Some of his dad's co-conspirators had been released and become family friends. And while they never gave blow-by-blow descriptions of their demise, they found ways to subtly convey his dad's role. But Danny wanted to hear it right from him, unfettered by the confines of a prison commissary or the spying eyes of prison staff. But all of those hopes were gone now.

What was worse to Danny, though, was that he held little hope of seeing his daddy in heaven either. Tears gathered in the corners of his eyes as he ran and contemplated this loss. And his face snarled as the adrenaline of the run and his emotions lengthened his stride. He had studied the Scriptures over and over. He desperately wanted to conclude that Christ's sacrifice was to save everyone regardless of their heart toward God. And, despite a couple of verses that when taken out of context seem to suggest this, he knew it wasn't the truth. As far as he knew, and as far as he would ever know, his dad didn't accept Christ. Of course, he reasoned, maybe something happened during those months he was shuffled from hospital to hospital. But he knew it was a pipedream. His dad's heart had been hardened by a lifetime of unbelief and decades of living in a cage. And even if he did somehow accept, there's no way Danny could ever know until he himself died.

As Danny turned on his street and headed home, he was compelled to ask God for the impossible—to save his dad anyway.

"God, I know what your Word says about this. I know that you're loving, but you're fair and just, too. In the end, I trust your judgment about my dad's soul. Whether he's with you now or not, I trust you and I accept your decision." He paused his prayer for a few seconds as he mustered the courage to ask, "But if there's any way you can save him, please do. If you can go back in time somehow and save him, I beg you. But I trust you. I trust you. I trust you."

As he repeated this over and over, the knot in his chest relaxed. A smile slowly came on his face, and his stride felt lighter. The pain of the run subsided and a peace about his dad's fate—the peace he read about in Scripture, that goes beyond understanding—settled on him. The tears in his eyes became tears of joy as he headed for home, ready to remember and celebrate Dave's life for what it was, ready to peacefully abide and move on to the next chapter of his life.

Chapter Two

A YEARNING

1977

Ecclesiastes 4:4 – And I saw that all toil and all achievement spring from one person's envy of another. This too is meaningless, a chasing after the wind.

The blaring horn to his left startled Dave from his zombie state, and he jerked the steering wheel to bring himself back into the lane. Mindless driving was the norm for this well-worn path, but his trance was particularly deep on this cold November evening. Dave flicked his cigarette butt out the narrow opening of his window then closed it.

Earlier in the day he and his best friend, Tom Brooks, who ran his auto-parts store in Roseland, had a tough discussion. Tom relayed that the addition of remanufactured parts to their offerings hadn't yielded the additional sales they expected. They were hemorrhaging money, over thirty-thousand for the year so far. The original Four Seasons Auto Parts on Stony Island was still doing well, but Dave could ill-afford to keep rolling those profits to the other store or taking more loans to expand the offerings. Tom volunteered to resign to save Dave the salary, but Dave told him to go to hell, no way that was going to happen. So the prospect of visiting his father to discuss another loan soaked up every bit of Dave's focus, save for the instinctual reactions to red lights and horns. But first, a stop at home.

"Hey, why so late?" Linda asked, standing at the counter fixing dinner plates.

"Had to stop at 112th to chat with Tom on the way home."

"Everything all right?"

But before Dave could even answer, he heard a huge thud. Leaping from the third stair and landing with a toy gun in his hand to face Dave, his tow-headed five-year-old Danny pulled the trigger and yelled "Bam, bam" at his daddy. Clutching his chest, Dave fell back against the door and slowly dropped down to the floor.

"You got me, buddy. Now come over here and rescue me," he clutched as if he were short of breath and in pain. Danny ran over, dropping the gun on the kitchen carpet, and gave his daddy a huge hug and a big kiss on his lips.

"That's more like it," Dave said.

"Okay you two, get on up here so we can eat."

Dave grabbed a tall glass bottle of Pepsi from the fridge, poured himself a cup and put the bottle in the empty 8-pack container on the floor before joining them. Everyone assumed their usual spots at the round kitchen table: Danny across from his mommy and Dave to his right, facing the windows. Danny used his fork to further separate his chicken from his green beans and especially from his mashed potatoes. He really missed his old divider plate. No risk of overlap with that.

"You really shouldn't slouch like that, Dave; it's not good for your back." Dave momentarily puffed his chest out, then slowly recoiled to slouching as he took bites of his food.

"What did you do today, Danny?" he asked.

"I went to school. I came home, played with my animals. I went outside with Pal."

"Where is Pal?" Dave asked.

"Oh s#it," Linda realized as she got up and went downstairs to let him in.

"What did you learn in kindergarten today?" he asked. Danny shrugged his shoulders. "If you didn't learn something, then you wasted your time there."

"I guess I learned how to count in Spanish. Uno. Dos. Tres. Quattro." He paused and looked up at the ceiling.

"Cinco," Dave coached.

"Cinco," Danny quickly followed. "That's all we learned so far."

Linda returned to the table as did Pal, who nosed up to Dave's waiting hand. They finished their dinner ritual, and Danny ran off to the basement to watch some TV. Dave picked at Danny's chicken remnants while Linda started cleaning up.

"I've got to run over to my mom and dad's tonight," he said. "Gotta talk with my dad about some business."

"Okay," Linda said, not caring enough about the details to ask.

Dave gnawed on a leg bone like a dog and with a half-full mouth, "You want to get away before the baby comes?" he asked.

"Absolutely. Where to?"

"I was thinking Acapulco. You can enjoy the beach; I can play a little poker."

"You know I love it there," she admitted. Linda had become accustomed to the trappings of upper-middle-classdom. Growing up in a blue-collar, save-for-a-rainy-day family, the relative wealth of Dave's business ventures and gambling escapades, as well as the benefits of travel, leisure and adventure, were just what her younger soul had yearned for. And Dave liked giving them to her. "But you better put Danny to bed before you go. You know how he loves it."

Dave handed his plate to Linda. "Is it eight already? Danny!" he called.

"Yeah!" he yelled from the basement.

"Time for bed!"

"Already? Can I have five more minutes?"

"I gotta leave, so if you want five more minutes, I won't be able to tuck you in."

Danny didn't hesitate. Right away, Dave heard the pitter-patter of Danny's feet on the hard tile floor, and soon the thumping of the stairs. He crept up next to Dave, who was still picking at his food, and looked at him with wide eyes and a big smile. He turned as if to run away, but he paused and waited.

"I'm…" Dave said in a deep, slow voice, not turning his head. Danny dashed around the corner and up the six stairs, waiting at the top.

"Going…" Dave continued as he got up and rounded the corner to see Danny standing on the red shag carpet; he giggled and took off to the end of the hall, disappearing with a jump onto his parents' huge bed.

"To…" Danny heard the stairs making their usual creaking sound.

"Get…" He was getting so close, Danny shook as he balled up in the fetal position.

"That…" He was right outside the door. Here it comes!

"Boyyyyy!" Dave jumped onto the bed and tackled Danny. He wrestled and tickled him, his stubble rough against Danny's face. Danny tried to tickle him back with little actual success. As usual, the ritual was over before it began.

"Okay," Dave said. "Brush your teeth and grab a book, and I'll read to you for a bit before bed."

Danny ran out of the room. On his way back, he was about to turn into his room to grab one of his books, but he decided to try a ploy instead.

"Daddy, I don't want a book tonight. Can you tell me more about the planets?"

Dave took a deep breath. It was hard to find time to read enough to stay ahead of Danny's curiosities. He searched for some topic or tidbit he could talk about, but his mental energies weren't conducive to it.

"Not tonight, honey. Daddy's tired, and I have to get going. Just pick a short book, okay?" Danny went to his room and picked the longest book he could find, hoping it would prolong the evening. But Dave read about half of it and then took Danny to bed.

The Continental always felt heavy and cumbersome going around the tree-lined curves of Knollwood Drive, but Dave didn't really notice. He turned and drove up the large circle driveway of his parents' house, the giant engine revving up as he pressed the gas to climb the steep grade. Stopping right in front of the door, he emerged and pressed the doorbell. The sound of Yorkie's bark mixing with the tubular bells.

When the big white door opened, he was greeted with his mom's beaming smile. "Well, this is a surprise," Alice exclaimed. "Hurry in before you catch cold."

He gave his mom a hug, feeling her soft body melt into his. Such an old, comforting feeling. "Yeah, I got to talk with Dad about one of the stores."

"He's out by the pool," she said. "Can I get you something to eat or drink?"

"No thanks, Ma." He handed her his jacket and turned with purpose, heading to the pool. As he slid open the door for the sunroom, he flipped the switch in his mind. His emotions detached, his face relaxed and he was solely immersed in the moment. He smelled the musty sunroom give way to chlorine as he opened the second sliding door to the huge pool room. The sounds of his sister Debbie playing with a friend in the pool and his brother Mike playing air hockey off in the game room barely caught his attention. The cavernous room with its large wooden beams and sliding glass door walls never ceased to amaze Dave. *Why couldn't I have had this growing up?* he briefly thought before refocusing on the task before him.

Off to his left, sitting in the usual spot at the end of his sprawling bar was Whitey, wearing his typical plain white t-shirt, smoking his Pall Malls. Ravaged by polio as a child, Whitey carried the scars of the disease—a withered arm, stilted gait and speech impediment. Amazing how a man with a third-grade education and such ailments could overcome and amass such a fortune.

"Hey sonny," Whitey welcomed. "What cha doin' here?"

Dave grabbed a bar stool a couple down from Whitey and turned it to face him. "Well, I need to talk with you about 112th."

"Yeah, is it going any better?" he asked.

Dave sensed a snarky tone in his voice which wasn't actually there. He cringed inside at the direction he knew this would go. A direction, ironically, he would unwittingly lead it. "Well, I was hoping to get another ten to get through the holidays."

Whitey held the smoking cigarette in his lips and leaned to his left to grab his wallet, pulling out a scrap of paper from the thick leather billfold. Studying it, he finally squeezed some words around the cig pursed in his lips, "That would bring you to thirty-five. I told you that place was going to be a money pit."

"Yeah, well, it's not, Dad," he snapped, his tone divulging his frustration. So much for his mental switch. It seldom worked with his dad. "We just need a little more time for the rebuilts to catch on. I'm going to take out an ad and put some flyers in the mail to the local shops. It will take off, I guarantee it."

"Seems like I heard that before."

"Come on, Pop, when have I ever not paid you back?" To his left he heard his name and he turned to see Debbie waving at him from the diving board. He waved and turned back. "Besides, Stony is still going strong. If need be, Linda and I can buckle down after the baby is born next year and pay you back from those profits."

Whitey put the wallet on the bar, got up and went around to the back to refresh his drink. "You want some Wild Turkey or something?"

"No, I don't have time," he lied. The sounds of his brother yelling in victory from the game room temporarily distracted him. Turning back to Whitey, "Whadya say? Can I get the loan?"

"Well, you know you've been spending pretty large the last couple of years, sonny. The pool, the cars, trips to Vegas and what not. You think you can rein it in if you need to pay me back?"

Whitey knew what Dave's answer would be. He didn't ask the question in order to hear the answer, but rather to read his body language. Likewise, Dave didn't take Whitey's question as a question, but a statement—you can't top me. No matter what Dave did, Whitey somehow stayed ahead of him. Dave got an Olympic-sized pool; Whitey got an Olympic-sized indoor pool with a game room. Dave opened another store; Whitey opened two more stores. A bitter feeling snuck into Dave's heart without it becoming conscious in his mind: *I regret dropping out of school to save your precious business!* And in the microsecond it took to register Whitey's question and formulate his response, Dave's face showed Whitey his true answer. So even though Dave told him "yes," Whitey shook his head.

"You need to rein it in now, sonny boy. Sorry."

Dave pursed his lips and nodded. "Okay, I guess I'll just figure it out some other way. Thanks anyway," he said with sarcasm. Dave walked back through the house to leave, the lights were all out but the room was still mildly illuminated by the lights from the pool shining across the yard through the windows. Down the long hallway he saw the TV light flickering off his mom's profile as she lay in bed.

"You going, Dave?" she yelled.

"Yeah, Mom."

"Take the pie in the fridge to Danny. It's his favorite, apple."

"Thanks Mom, he'll love that." He grabbed the pie. "Love you," he said as he put on his jacket and left for home.

Returning home, he walked in the house, kitchen lights still on. Linda was in the front room reading. He peeked around the corner, "Hey."

"Hey," she said back. "How'd it go?"

"Fine," he embellished, keeping his life suitably compartmentalized. "I'm gonna go down and watch some TV before bed."

"Okay, I may join you in a bit."

Dave went down to his tiny bar and poured himself a Chivas Regal. Without itemizing everything, he judged the room: crappy wood paneling, low ceiling, tiny fridge. At least his recliner was nice and comfortable. He sank into it and opened the cigar box to his right. He put some tobacco in his pipe and took a few drags, wincing as he washed it down with a swig of whiskey.

The "MASH" theme song played on the TV, but it offered him no distraction from his thoughts. The ambulance lights from the hospital out back didn't catch his eye as they resonated in the glass-block windows over the TV. *There has to be a way*, he thought. But he was tired of rehashing the same old ideas: sell the store, open another, take a partner, go to a bank, blah, blah, blah.

He took the last sip of whiskey and finally began to feel the effects of the alcohol and tobacco. As he was sinking into the relaxation of the buzz, a new idea began to emerge. It crystallized slowly like what happens when you stare at a 3D picture. A piece here comes into view, but if you try to focus on it, it goes away. It's only when you relax that the picture gets revealed. And so it was for Dave that night.

There was a way. But it was risky. It could bring him the wealth his heart desired. But it could be his undoing. "I would have to be very careful," he said in a low hushed tone. "Very careful."

Then he heard Linda's feet coming down the stairs, and it shook him from his trance. *It's a stupid idea*, he thought. *Too risky*. And he put it out of his mind. Or at least, he tried.

Chapter Three

WRONG TURN

1978

1 Timothy 6:9 – Those who want to get rich fall into temptation and a trap and into many foolish and harmful desires that plunge people into ruin and destruction.

The air was heavy and drizzle was beginning to fall as Dave took off his sport coat and threw it in the trunk along with his bag. It was almost dark as he ran around and got in the passenger seat. Tom Brooks was driving, and in the back seat was Ken Schaeffer, Tom's neighbor.

"D@mn, I miss Vegas weather already," Dave said.

Tom didn't even look at him; he just peered over the round silver rim of his glasses to his side mirror, turned on his signal and pulled away from the madhouse of O'Hare. "So, how'd you do?" he asked.

"Another thirty successfully cleaned. I lost my shirt though. How about you two? Tell me about Kansas City."

"It's a s#it hole," Ken chimed in, "but the coke is good."

"Hopefully you learned a little more than that."

"Come on, you jagoff!" Tom shouted at a taxi as he blared his horn. He moved swiftly to the left lane and accelerated, then his tone lightened, "You wouldn't believe this s#it, Dave. This conference felt like some legitimate business meeting or something. You would never guess it was to teach people how to run drugs and stuff. Totally unreal."

Dave put a cigarette in a plastic mouthpiece intended to filter the tar and such from it. He lit it up and cracked the window in the Towncar. "What kind of numbers were they talking?"

"They had some guys who were running about four to five hundred pounds of reefer each week," Tom replied.

Ken closed his eyes in the backseat and rested his fat head against the headrest. Dave did some quick mental calculations. "So that's 150k gross, right? What's the profit?"

"Depends on where you get it. If you run a boat out to the mother ship, you can get it for $150 per pound. If you get it from someone who imports it, it costs closer to $250."

"$250?" Dave questioned. "That's ridiculous. By the time you get it to Chicago, you'll eat up the spare fifty in cost. You'll barely break even."

"There's a lot of variables, Dave," Tom responded. "It depends on the quality of the stuff, how motivated the seller is, who's transporting it. Plus, you can get into coke. It's easier to move and more profitable."

Dave loved the idea of bigger numbers, but the thought of getting into cocaine made him squirm. It was one thing to consider bringing in pot; that was as harmless as liquor in his mind. But something about coke was a line he wasn't willing to cross. At least, not yet.

"No coke," he barked. "We're not going there."

"I'm going there," Ken chimed in. The word coke must have jarred him from his stupor.

Dave turned around and gave Ken his "no joke" stare. The piercing gaze was normally reserved for troublesome employees or to intimidate during high-stakes business deals. "You do what you want. You're not a part of what we're doing here."

"Fine by me," replied Ken as he shut his eyes and laid his head back again.

Dave turned back toward Tom. "If I'm going to get into this, it has to be big. I don't want to screw around for thousands. And, we need to get the Outfit's permission. You heard Jimmy got whacked, right?"

"Ed told me. What happened?"

"Not sure. These things happen all the time. I need to talk with Ostrowski to see if this changes my arrangement. I'm getting sick of these Vegas trips. I don't know why I agreed to do them." But Dave did know why he agreed to it: He loved the idea of being connected. His whole life, he'd been fascinated by the mob—the structure, the power, the respect. And the recent attention by Hollywood just made the prospect of getting involved, even as a lackey, all the more enticing.

Still, the prospect of going deeper like he and Tom were planning gave Dave pause. He debated whether to say the next thought that popped into his mind. It sounded cheesy and sensational to him, but deep down, he was afraid it really wasn't. "You know, if we really do this, we're going to have to be real careful. Moving parts and cleaning money is one thing, but this is another. These guys don't play around. If we step on the wrong toes or screw something up, it could be the end for us."

Tom slowly exhaled the smoke from his last puff and put his cigarette out in the ashtray. "Well," he said, matter-of-factly, "we'll just have to be careful then." And they both just nodded their heads.

Steve moved the lever on the steering column to park and shut off the headlights. Dave was a bit surprised to be having this meeting at a restaurant, especially a Lithuanian one on the east side. But maybe that's why it was genius.

"Now remember," Steve said in his coarse tone, "you gotta be careful to not offend him. Be real polite and respectful."

Dave replied with a hint of annoyance, "Yeah, yeah, I got it. Call him sir, don't stare him down."

Steve's advice was good. By all rights, Steve could pistol-whip Dave right then for the hacked-off tone he was using with him. If he did that with Albert Tocco, there's no telling what might happen. "Look, you can be pretty intense when the stakes are high. I've seen it. I'm just trying to help you out," Steve added.

They simultaneously opened the car doors and stepped into the cold night air. Dave's breath looked like smoke as it came from his mouth. His heart was beating harder than he expected, so he took an extra deep breath as they headed through the heavy wooden door.

Inside, the lighting was dim and the air smelled of fried potatoes. Dave scanned the room looking to see if he could spot the mob boss. There was a tall, well-dressed, dark-haired guy with his back to them at the bar. *That's probably not him*, he thought. There was a Mexican family seated in the middle and an elderly couple. *Strange to see an elderly couple dining at this hour*, he thought. But the most alarming sight were the two cops seated near the entrance, sipping their coffees. Dave wondered if their meeting would be canceled with them there. Or maybe they were on the take. Either way, Dave didn't see anyone fitting his stereotype of Albert Tocco.

Walking toward them came a stout, comely lady with her gray hair up in a bun. In a thick accent, she welcomed, "Hallo Ostrich. You here to eat or see da boss?"

"Mr. Tocco's expecting us, Darla."

"Okay," she said as she did an about-face and headed over to the bar. She spoke to the tall man at the bar who looked back toward them. Steve waved. The man didn't wave back.

Dave got a smirk and slowly turned his head toward Steve. "Ostrich?"

"Mr. Tocco likes to give people nicknames for some reason."

The well-dressed man got up and walked toward a door near the back of the room and went inside. Dave looked down at his attire and felt like he was suitably dressed for the part—gold cufflinks and Italian shoes. His large shirt collar flared out over the jacket with his top two buttons open. He looked at his reflection in the beer sign on the wall and straightened some thin stray hairs which escaped his comb-over. His blonde hair looked particularly dark in the dim light. A few minutes later, the young man came back out and walked over to them. Looking over to the cops, he pointed toward the front door. Dave took the hint and walked outside.

"Arms up," he ordered, and Dave was confused. *Is he robbing me?* He looked over to Steve.

"He wants to make sure you ain't packing," Steve explained.

Dave lifted his arms out, and the guy felt along his sides and his back. Dave typically carried a gun when he was away from home. There were certain risks a white man endured in owning a business in the ghetto. But he realized it unwise to bring one to this meeting. After feeling around each ankle, the man stood up and headed back in. Steve followed suit and Dave brought up the rear as they sauntered to the door in the back of the room.

Walking through the doorway was like entering into another world. The room was dark, the ceiling was tall, and there was only one round table set toward the back. The sole light in the room was a hanging lamp directing light on the table where two men sat talking. As his eyes adjusted, he could make out two doors on his left. The walls were plain white with a wooden chair-rail about a quarter of the way up. Otherwise, the room was very plain, impersonal. The men were wrapping up their discussion as the three of them stood and waited their turn.

The tone of their conversation was light, which brought Dave some comfort. He would hate to follow up a tense conversation. The man facing them had thick, dark hair combed back with a part. His head was large and his eyes intense. He assumed this was Tocco, positioned to see the entry and in close proximity to the side door. *A likely escape route*, he surmised. The visitor stood up and walked around to Tocco and gave him a manly hug. Tocco was shorter than Dave expected, but his stout build projected strength through his tight suit coat. The man left through the side door and then the fun began.

Tocco looked over at them, specifically at his handler. "Come on, Marco," he invited, waving them over.

The ten steps to the table felt like one as Dave's mind raced with doubt. *Should I really do this? Is it too late to turn around?* It was. Dave flipped his mental switch.

"Ostrich," Tocco said as he walked up to the two of them, coming almost uncomfortably close. Marco had peeled off and stood to the side of the room between the two doors.

"Mr. Tocco, thank you for this meeting, sir. This is Dave Domberg."

Dave extended his hand and Tocco grabbed hold, his grip tight and his eyes projecting friendliness, confidence. "Mr. Tocco, I appreciate you taking the time to meet with us tonight."

"Of course," he affirmed with a smile. "Ostrich, would you please wait outside? Mr. Domberg, please have a seat."

Steve looked dumbfounded and hesitated for a couple of seconds before replying, "Yes, sir. I...I'll be having a drink outside."

Out of instinct, Dave sat in the same seat as the last visitor, directly facing Tocco. As he settled in, he felt right at home, like he was about to engage in a game of poker. The light overhead brought a very narrow focus to the scene.

"So, Mr. D, you mind if I call you Mr. D?" Tocco asked as he pulled a cigar out of the inside pocket of his coat.

"Of course," Dave said, glad his new nickname wasn't something like ostrich.

Tocco continued. "You like cigars?"

"I like all kinds of tobacco," he admitted. He noticed he was slouching and he heard Linda's voice in his head telling him to straighten up. But he resisted the urge. He figured slouching would be a more submissive posture.

Tocco handed the cigar across the table and took another from his pocket. Dave smelled it and studied the foil—Cuban. He bit off the end and they lit up. The smell began to permeate the room.

"So, Ostrich tells me you're doing good work for us with the chop shop operations. You're clearing some parts and some money for us, huh?"

"Yes sir. I really appreciate being able to help out."

"How much you move this year?" Albert asked, already knowing the answer.

"It's just over two-forty so far."

"Yeah, and what do you take from that?"

"I get five," answered Dave.

"Wow," exclaimed Tocco, the wrinkles in his forehead appearing as his eyes widened, "you must be a d@mn good negotiator, Mr. D. Five points is rare."

"I don't know about that, sir," Dave said, lowering his eyes.

"Oh yeah," Tocco continued, his voice getting louder. "You've got quite the reputation." Tocco's eyes got narrow and he stared at Dave, letting silence linger.

Dave worried this was going in a bad direction, and he swallowed the lump in his throat. If this was poker, he was being tested to see what his reaction would be under stress. He did his best to remain in his slouched posture as he took a puff from his cigar.

"Ostrich tells me you had a fire at one of your stores this summer," Tocco continued.

"Yeah, it was a total loss. But there's always a silver lining with these things," he answered with a smirk.

"Are they still investigating it?"

"I don't think so, sir. I got the fire marshal from another district to get involved, and I think he's got it put to bed. Took him on a junket to Vegas."

Dave looked at the growing ash at the end of his cigar and flicked it into the tray. He wanted to get on to the main topic. He tried to imagine just blurting out, "So can I bring drugs up here or what?" But he knew this was more than just a business meeting.

"I hear you got a new pool last summer…" Dave was surprised he would know that, but his face remained expressionless as he nodded his head. "Your little boy must really love it."

A shadow crossed his heart as he considered that Danny might somehow get intertwined with this plan of his. "Yes, sir. It's kind of a big deal with our friends and family."

Tocco exhaled slowly, savoring the flavor. "Family is important," he agreed, nodding his head. "I have a brother, Mr. D. Do you have a brother?"

Dave nodded.

"My brother Joey is…" Tocco paused, searching for the right words, "causing me some grief, Mr. D. He always wants to be involved in my business, but he's not the sharpest knife in the drawer." He spoke in a low tone with an air of seriousness to it. "I give him jobs, but I always got to keep an eye on him, you know?"

Dave nodded again, not knowing what to say.

"Like right now, he's gummed up a load of liquor we brought in under the radar. Truck got caught doing deliveries in Hegwish, and the products had no tax stamps. Joey spent a few days in Cook before we got him bailed out."

Dave was struggling to see the point of this.

"While he was in there," Tocco continued, "he apparently said some things that some guards overheard. Stuff that could really hurt my business, you know? My bosses are wanting me to fix this, obviously, but I'm struggling to figure out the right way to handle it."

Dave realized what was going on. He tried to envision the right response, but he found himself talking before his ideas coalesced. "It seems to me you have two options. You can bribe the guards to keep their mouths shut or you can have them whacked."

Albert set his cigar in the ashtray, nodding his head. "You misunderstand, Mr. D. I know how to handle that. What I'm struggling with is what to do about my brother."

The gravity of the conversation overtook Dave. He paused for a few seconds, running through scenarios, trying to discern the best approach. Not wanting to look uncertain, he decided to take the safe route.

"Well, he'd be out of the business, for sure. Probably have make him clean up his own mess somehow. Make sure he's scared enough to keep quiet."

Tocco looked down for a second; when he looked up, the expression on his face had changed. It was a relaxed, almost disinterested look. "So, Ostrich tells me you'd like to bring some products up here. What kinds?"

"Well, pot for sure," he answered. "We have some connections in Florida."

"Who's we?" Tocco asked, sounding a bit skeptical.

"My right hand is an ex-cop, Tom Brooks. Close friend. Smart."

"Uh huh. And how much you thinking about bringing in?"

"I want to go big. My hope is to get it up to five mil within a year or so." Dave was momentarily distracted as he reflected on his use of the word hope. "I know we can get at least that," he said more confidently.

"Uh huh," Tocco said again. His open mouth and blank expression reflected his skepticism. "And who's gonna move it once it's up here?"

"I'm planning to use a bunch of guys. We'll pound it out and get it to the gangs and others who are hungry for more than Cooper is getting them right now." Dave purposely mentioned Cooper to show Tocco he'd done his homework too. "I'd assume he's at risk given what happened to Catura."

Tocco's unblinking expression changed to mildly impressed. "Yeah, things are definitely in a state of, shall we say, flux right now. But something's puzzling me, Mr. D. You got a good business going. You're doing some work for us now, and you're doing good. It's low risk. You're on the outside so there's none of the hassle that comes with being inside the Outfit. Why would a nice Swedish boy like you want to get mixed up in this s#it?"

This was a question Dave was ready for. He tried unsuccessfully to not sound rehearsed. "Well sir, I know I can do more. I know I can be more, if I can just get in the right organization. I've helped my father build our businesses pretty much on my own. I see potential that others miss. Yeah, I've got a pretty good, comfortable life. But some people aren't wired for peace and comfort. I'm gonna do something bigger. And more importantly, I want to help you do the same thing."

Tocco stared at Dave as if waiting for him to continue. He shifted his weight in his chair. Dave's heart raced with adrenaline. "Well Mr. D, you're obviously a smart man. It was wise of you to come to see me about this. Let me give you some advice. You can't handle what you're trying to get into."

Dave's expression turned serious, and he matched Tocco's stare as Tocco continued in a very intense, provocative tone, "You're a white boy from the suburbs who's been successful because your daddy got you started. You never had to fight for your life. You never lived in the jungle. Good! Go back to your family and be happy. You got vacations, a pool, nice cars. Stay in the shallow waters where the sharks don't swim. Trust me, you can't handle it."

If this were the old west, Dave would have drawn his gun. This was no longer a poker game. His jaw clenched as he resisted his base urges. Finally, he came back to the moment and re-flipped his switch.

"With all due respect, Mr. Tocco, your assessment of me is wrong. I wasn't handed everything by my father. I had to drop out of school to run our businesses when I was sixteen, on my own. I didn't grow up in the 'burbs, I grew up in Beverly and I've spent most of my life on State and Marquette. I'm not in the jungle because I mow the jungle down and build on it. I've got cops and aldermen in my pocket. I think I've proved myself with the chop business. But I know I can't do *this* without your permission. So I'm asking, can we please work together?"

Tocco was mildly impressed again. He sat back with his hand over his mouth, holding back his words. He took a deep breath, his cheeks inflating as he exhaled. Finally he dropped his hand. "I tell you what, Mr. D. I like you," he paused, "so my answer is still no."

Dave's face betrayed his disappointment. He gave it his best shot. There was no point in arguing. He would have to figure out another way. He stood up and extended his hand. "Thank you for your time Mr. Tocco."

They shook hands. Dave turned around and began walking back to the restaurant where Steve was waiting. Tocco had saved Dave from himself. But only for a moment.

"You know Mr. D…you're right about Cooper." Dave stopped in his tracks, his back remaining to Tocco. "He's vulnerable. Unprotected. So as I see it, you got as much right to that market as he does. No one in my group will get in your way. If you can do what you think you can do, maybe we can talk again someday."

A green light. It was almost as good as hearing "welcome to the family." For the first time that day, Dave smiled.

Chapter Four

OUT OF HAND

1979

1 Peter 5:8 – Be alert and of sober mind. Your enemy the devil prowls around like a roaring lion looking for someone to devour.

Dave hadn't been sleeping well, so the loud ringing sound dragging him from the depths of dreamland was even more painful than usual. He slowly uncoiled his body and rolled over to his back side. 5:04 taunted him in red LED as if from hell itself. He groaned, but soon realized that a call at this hour was likely to be bad news. Linda began to stir. Quickly rolling to his right, he answered.

"Hello." He sounded like he was still drunk.

"Dave, we got a problem." Tom didn't sound tired or drunk. He sounded desperate. *Something must have gone wrong with the load,* he thought. Knowing he couldn't go into detail with his wife listening in, he cut it short.

"Ok. I'll be there in thirty minutes." And he hung up the phone.

"What's going on?" Linda asked, rubbing her eyes.

"Another break-in," Dave answered. "I gotta get to the store."

"Jesus," she complained in a tired whisper, and she closed her eyes.

Dave got dressed without a shower, brushed his teeth, grabbed some coffee and headed to the car. He ran through his mind all that could be wrong. *Who did Tom use for this load? Did they get busted while getting it? Did they get robbed? Or killed?* These were not friendly people they were dealing with. He backed out of his house, took the short drive down the block and pulled into Tom's circle driveway. Without delay, Tom ran out to the car.

"I would say good morning, but I'd guess this isn't a good morning."

"Yeah, you could say that." Tom looked gaunt and tired. "I got a call from Harry an hour ago. I sent him and Billy down to pick up our load. On the way up here, they got pulled over by an agricultural inspector." Tom took a puff from his cigarette.

"S#it," Dave blurted in a fairly calm voice.

"Yeah, and it gets worse. Harry freaked out and pulled a gun on the guy. He and Billy took him to some church in the sticks and tied him up."

The gravity of the situation began to sink in. Dave covered his face with his hands and muttered, "Ohhh, s#it."

Tom continued, "They dumped the load and swapped plates on the truck, and they're holed up in some backwoods motel in west Florida."

The words "dumped the load" caught Dave's attention. And his ire. "They dumped the load? What do you mean they dumped the d@mn load?"

"Like I said, they freaked out. They figure the heat's on so they took the topper off the truck, dumped the load in the woods and got out of there."

Dave turned and met Tom's eyes. "First of all, why in the hell did you send your moron brothers down there? I warned you about this. Second, we can't just dump eighty grand in the forest."

Tom nodded his head and looked away from Dave. He was afraid his eyes would give him away. "I know," he said. "We gotta get that load back. Gotta calm the boys down. I should get on a flight."

"We got to slow down and think," Dave demanded in a deliberate, stern voice. "Going too fast will only get us in more trouble. Son of a bitc#, Tom. We were just getting in a groove."

"I'll clean this up, Dave, I just need some help."

"Let's back up a minute. This inspector, is he still tied up?"

"As far as I know," Tom replied.

"That guy needs to be bribed. Or threatened. Or both. Then you need to get the load. We'll need another vehicle. Do you know if this inspector reported the truck before he was kidnapped?"

"I got no idea."

"We'll have to assume he did. I suppose their plates are traceable to them?" Dave asked with a look of disappointment.

Meekly, Tom replied, "Yeah."

"Tom, Tom, Tom. I thought we talked about this. You gotta keep more separation. You gotta keep yourself safe."

"I know," Tom admitted with frustration, "we screwed this up! But we gotta figure out what to do now!"

Tom's beeper blared, and he looked down. "This is probably Harry again; let's go inside and give him a call back."

"No," Dave retorted, pulling out of the driveway. "We're heading to the store first. We need to be able to talk freely."

"He's freaking out, Dave!"

"He'll have to wait!"

In order to be successful at running a criminal enterprise, one must be good at compartmentalizing. Partners, lackeys, buyers, sellers, authorities and family must be kept in their respective lanes, sharing with them only the information necessary for them to accomplish their task. Give them too much information and you run the risk they'll say the wrong thing to the wrong person and bring the whole operation down. Layers and buffers are key. Your right-hand man might only know half of what's really going on. His right hand man only fifty percent of that. By the time you get down to the lackeys, they're not even sure who the real head of the organization is.

This was Dave's game, and he was pretty good at it. But the kidnapping of the agricultural inspector, Leonard Pease, brought the complexity of the situation to another level. There were a lot of variables to keep track of, a lot of options to consider. Should they bribe Pease to keep the Brooks brothers out of jail? If that didn't work, how could they keep them from ratting out Dave and Tom in order to reduce their sentences? What about the $80,000 load that was ditched? Could they recover it? Who did he trust enough to involve in the recovery and bribe? How could he protect himself in case it all went bad?

To complicate things further, Dave didn't know all the variables in play. Even the best chess player can't win if they don't have all the pieces. What Dave didn't know, what Tom didn't tell him, was the load wasn't $80,000. It was $130,000. Tom and another of their clan, Sam, pooled together some money and started a side business of their own, piggy-backing on Dave's. Sam talked Tom into it when he began to doubt Dave's bluster of being connected to the Outfit. He reasoned that they were taking all the risk and doing all the work. So why not reap the rewards? Apparently, there really is no honor amongst thieves, even when you're best friends.

So not only did Tom have to deal with the kidnapping and recovery, but he had the added complications of keeping their secret and protecting his brothers. And Tom was not as good as Dave at dealing with complex, intertwined deceptions.

Dave enlisted the help of Jim, a cop friend of theirs who was involved in the organization, and Ed McCabe, another friend and partner. Jim, Ed and Tom met up with Harry in Atlanta. The younger brother Bill had been sent off to Austin, Texas, because the truck was registered in his name and by the time they got there the heat was on.

The plan was originally to bribe and threaten Pease, recover the load and get the brothers into hiding for a while. But as fate would have it, Pease was found before they even had a chance to get there. A lady visited that church early the next morning and called the authorities.

The countryside was crawling with cops looking for Bill and Harry, and the pot. So, unbeknownst to Dave, Tom and the crew hatched a plan to use Ed's plane to survey the area where they dumped the load. Once it was found, Tom and Harry rented a van and recovered it while Ed and Jim watched from the sky. If cops were getting close, they would drop down and "crop dust" them as a warning.

While hatching their plan, they brainstormed their options for Bill and Harry now that Pease had been found. At this point a bribe was unrealistic; no way Pease would take it. That left two options: Bill and Harry turn themselves in and take their lumps, or Leonard Pease dies. All the Brookses wanted the latter. Tom agreed to broach the topic with Dave when he got back. Maybe his connections with the Outfit could be of help.

Through all of this, per the plan, Tom maintained radio silence with Dave. But, as the days stacked up, Dave's normally stoic demeanor began to fray. And when Tom finally returned to Four Seasons Auto Parts, the powder keg was bound to blow.

Dave looked down through the large picture windows perched above the front lobby of the auto parts store. He tried to balance the ledger but he couldn't seem to get it right. His eyes flashed to the front door whenever he sensed the slightest motion. He'd been waiting there for hours since Tom called him.

Finally walking through the glass entry door, Tom looked up to see Dave's scowling face. He went quickly to the stairs on his left and bounded up the narrow corridor. Perched at the top, Jim Sheldon, an off-duty cop and friend, acted as deterrent for theft and robberies. Tom didn't even hear or acknowledge Jim's greeting as he went by. He was singularly focused.

Tom opened the door to the outer office to Dave's right. The music playing in the store got louder and caught Dave's ear: Rod Stewart singing Do Ya Think I'm Sexy. Any other occasion and that earworm would have eaten away in his mind the rest of the day. But it was out of Dave's consciousness seconds later as Tom walked through the second inner-office door, the hinges squeaking as the door gingerly opened.

Dave didn't turn around to look at Tom. He kept writing in the ledger as he started. "Close the door," he ordered. Tom closed it as gently as he opened it. "What day is it, Tom?"

Tom looked down onto Dave's balding head. "Uhh, it's Tuesday, I guess."

Dave nodded his head. "Uh huh, and what day did you leave?

"Sorry, Dave. I was going to call you, but the situation was more complicated than we expected. I didn't want to risk anything more."

Tom walked over to the desk to Dave's left and had a seat in the chair. Dave turned his head to look at him, then turned his whole chair to face him, his elbows resting on armrests and hands steepled in front of his face. "Okay, tell me what happened then."

"Well, the inspector got found before we could get to him. The news has got it all over the place down there. Bill's and Harry's names all over the news. We had to think on our feet. We decided to recover the load and get them out of the hot zone."

"So you got the load at least?" Dave felt a measure of relief as Tom nodded his head.

"I got it at my place. My old man is helping to split it up."

"Where are the knuckleheads?" Dave asked.

Tom looked back up and met Dave's eyes. "Look man, I'm really worried about them. I mean, it's bad enough they got an APB out for them. They're freaking out. They need help, and they're scared s#itless that you won't protect them."

This was a pivotal moment for Dave. He surmised their fear was as much about getting into trouble with the Outfit as it was getting into trouble with the law. He visualized the situation with all its variables and tried to see a path where everyone came out clean. He couldn't find one. Down one path, he could fess up to Tom and his "organization"—let them know there's no mob connection. They might still figure out a way to get to a politician or prosecutor and get the charges reduced. Down that path was humiliation and the death of wealth and power. Down another path, he could double down. He would continue to leverage the perception of his pseudo-mob involvement and stoke their fear to keep Bill and Harry in line. Another fork in the road for Dave. Another chance to right this story.

"I don't know if I *can* protect them, Tom. But we've got to get together to figure out what we can do. They can't live the rest of their lives on the run from this now that the law is involved. In all likelihood, they'll have to turn themselves in and pay for this mistake."

Tom shook his head. "Look, I love my brothers, but you know they don't have the strongest backbones, especially Billy. You gotta figure out another way. Can't Tocco help us out here? He's gotta have connections to help us out with this Pease guy. We..."

"We," Dave interrupted loudly, "ain't involving Tocco. Think about it, Tom. What's lower risk for him, offing a law enforcement officer or offing your brothers?"

Silence lingered for a moment as that reality registered for Tom. "Can we do it ourselves then? Ed says he won't do it, but he knows this other guy who might."

Dave shook his head. "I'm willing to help get your brothers out of this mess, Tom, but if anyone's getting whacked, it's them. I told you to keep them on the selling side, not the big stuff, because s#it like this could happen. Now we gotta prepare them for their options."

"Harry said if you don't help him out, then he's gonna blow it up."

"Is he really that dumb, Tom? He's going to threaten me?" His face winced with disbelief.

Tom interrupted, "He's just freaking out. But I really think you should just hire a guy to off Pease. I would think ten grand would be a small price to protect us all."

"Here's what you're going to do," Dave's voice and facial expressions reflected the finality of this statement, "you're going to get me in contact with your brothers and we're going to convince them to turn themselves in. It's their best move. I can use my political connections to see if we can get a good judge. I might even be willing to try another bribe for this Pease guy. But at the end of the day, you put them in the position, they took the risk, and now they need to pay for it, one way or another. You and I and they would much rather have them pay for it with a little jail time versus the alternative. Don't you agree?"

Tom took a deep breath and nodded. This didn't go the way he had planned. But it seldom ever did with Dave.

In the weeks that followed, Tom and Dave did their best to make Bill and Harry see that this was their best option. But the Brooks brothers disagreed. To them, the best plan was to eliminate Pease from the equation. Without his testimony, there would be no way to positively tie them to the kidnapping. So they hatched a plan to do just that.

Ed McCabe knew a guy named Joe, a steelworker and thug from Chicago who was known to do dirty deeds. Ed got Tom and Joe together, and they made a deal. Ten thousand dollars, which Tom and Sam contributed from the profits of their side business, was the going rate for knocking off someone in law enforcement. Joe seemed a little unstable, which gave Tom some second thoughts about their plan. But Tom figured you had to be a little crazy to do what they were asking him to do. And, his lack of faith in his brothers' ability to keep quiet made this the only feasible way of saving their lives he could conjure.

On the night of April 15th, 1979, an agricultural inspector was murdered with one gunshot wound to the back of the head. His body was found a week later, covered in a tarp, naked and decaying. When news of the murder hit the airwaves, as Tom knew it eventually would, his heart sank. He wasn't troubled by the evil they perpetrated. It sank because he realized that his brothers were not out of trouble at all. Leonard Pease would still be able to testify against them. Leonard Pease was not killed that night. Austin Dewey Gay was.

As Tom looked around the table at the faces of his father and his brothers, head in his hands, all he could say was, "Well, we better get our story together."

Chapter Five

TOO BIG FOR HIS BRITCHES

1982

Proverbs 16:18 – Pride goes before destruction, a haughty spirit before a fall.

They say Lady Luck favors the bold. Whether that's true or not is debatable. What's not debatable is that she could care less about one's motives.

The wrong inspector was killed. But that murder went unsolved. It was never connected to the Pease kidnapping. Bill and Harry were convinced to turn themselves in. Dave pulled some political strings and got their sentences reduced for guilty pleas. That and their fear of the mob kept them sufficiently quiet and protected Dave's organization. They served their time like good soldiers.

The whole debacle caused Dave enough grief that he lowered his ambitions. Interviews with the FBI, scrutiny on his business and a triple bypass at thirty-four years old, will do that to you. Rather than expand into importation and growing into million dollar loads, he kept it smaller and more manageable. He slowed down and was more careful about who he brought into the fold.

Even though Dave didn't fully realize his goals on the monetary side, he was becoming more and more connected politically with both elected officials and with those in the underground. With that, he grew more and more confident in his ability to wield his power and influence to achieve his aims. One might say he was becoming a bit too confident. Rubbing shoulders with politicians and celebrities brings with it an aphrodisiac irresistible to all but sociopaths and saints. And of course, Dave was neither of those.

Gatherings in the Dombergs' backyard were common. Having a giant in-ground pool with slide and diving board made it the obvious fun spot. Every week, family and friends dropped by, sometimes unexpectedly. And each year the pinnacle of backyard bashes happened on the Fourth of July with fireworks and food aplenty. It was an annual spectacle which taught Danny just how a party is really supposed to look—horseshoe tournaments, belly flops, pool volleyball, music and mayhem. You had to have your head on a swivel, for at any moment one of the Manning brothers could grab you, hoist you over their shoulder and lob you safely into the water. No one was off limits, not even Grandma; although her lobs were more like how you'd lower a baby into a bath versus the awkward and forceful plunges others received.

But this Fourth of July was particularly exciting for Danny for completely different reasons. This year, there would be a special guest.

Six weeks earlier, he way laying on the couch in the basement when his dad came down to give him a kiss and hug goodbye.

"Where are you going?" Danny asked. Dave hesitated and replied that he was just going to have dinner with some friends. "Why you dressed up in your suit?" he prodded.

"Well, we're going to a fancy restaurant." If Dave had been a bit more self-aware, he would have blunted the conversation right there. But part of him really wanted to tell Danny.

"Who's going with you?" Danny asked, curious as usual.

"Well," Dave dragged out the sentence like he didn't want to say, "I'm actually going to preview the new Rocky movie with my friend I told you about, Mr. T..." Had the sentence ended there, it would have been bad enough. But he just couldn't contain his pride. "...and afterward we're going to dinner with Sylvester Stallone."

There are a million things much more consequential Dave could have said there. He could have said "You're going to have another brother." Or, "I'm leaving the family and I don't know if I'll ever see you again." Or, "Reagan just launched nukes at Russia." But nothing could have elicited the mixture of manic excitement and overwhelming anguish that followed.

Rocky was more than just a movie for Danny, it was a revelation. It was fast becoming part of his personality; a secondary persona he could call upon when his self-esteem was waning. So Dave should have known better. As Danny's pleas went from hope and awe to heartbreak and tears, Dave did his best to console. None of it worked. Danny's blood raced through his veins and rationality was out the window. Finally, out of desperation, Dave went out on a limb and promised that Mr. T would come to their Fourth of July party.

"Who cares?" Danny shouted, as he stormed off to his room. Danny didn't know who this Mr. T guy was. It wasn't Rocky. It wasn't even Apollo. He stewed in his room for hours.

But after seeing the movie on opening day, everything changed. Rocky's hulking foe, Clubber Lang, was so mean and tough. At nine years old, Danny couldn't imagine what it would be like to see him in person. Would he make his snarling face and challenge Danny to a fight? Would he say, "I pity the fool who likes Balboa"?

The days counted down like weeks. He imagined he might actually get to box with Clubber; so he trained every day, donning his boxing gloves and punching the heavy bag in the garage, or his younger brother Dougie.

That's what he was doing as the day finally arrived. In the early morning, to vent his pent up excitement, he and his brother, Dougie, re-enacted the "Rocky III" fight scenes on Dougie's bed. As Danny pummeled his four-year-old brother, an explosion rocked the house. Throwing off the gloves with a wave of his hands, Danny ran out of the room, through their parents' room and out to the sun porch to see what happened. Looking down, he saw the unmistakable frame of his Uncle Mark. His six feet four inches looked tall to Danny, even from up on the second floor. Mark turned to look up at them with a boyish grin, satisfied with their glowing, startled faces. Nothing like an M80 outside your window to kick off the party to end all parties.

His early arrival showed that Danny wasn't the only one looking forward to this occasion. A lot of people got there early that day, and the crowd grew larger than normal. The music, the laughter, the smoke billowing from the grill, the sunshine—it was a perfect day. Perfect except for the anticipation. He stayed close by his daddy, knowing the first signs of arrival would come through him. Despite admonishments and outright orders to go and play with his best friends or to go and swim in the pool, he seldom let Dave out of his sight. Every time Dave's pager beeped, Danny's eyes lit up like Pavlov's dogs. After a while, he began to preempt Danny's begging question. "It's not him, Danny. Go and play."

It wasn't unusual for Dave's pager to beep often. But one of the pages coming through repeatedly that day was from a number Dave didn't recognize. Given his state of affairs, he ignored it a couple of times. But when it came through a third time, he couldn't avoid his curiosity any longer. *Maybe T is calling to cancel?* He dreaded the thought. Walking upstairs to his bedroom, sat on the edge of his bed and dialed. Dave didn't recognize the voice that answered.

"Hello. This is Dave Domberg. You've been paging me."

"Dave! This is Gary Allmon, you remember me, I assume?"

Gary Allmon was Dave and Tom's old pot connection in Florida. Over the six months of operation before the Pease kidnapping, they moved some thousand pounds over six loads. Dave had met Gary a couple of times and even spoke with him over the phone a few times, but it was always all business. After the Pease load, Gary admonished him and Tom to stay away for a while and let things cool off. They did. When they eventually got back into operation, they used other sources, figuring they'd burned that bridge with Gary. Hearing his voice again brought back old memories and a twinge of PTSD.

"Yeah, Gary, of course. What's going on?"

"Well, I have a business opportunity I think you might be interested in. I remember you saying you wanted to get into big deals...importing and stuff. You ever get that off the ground?"

"You know, Gary, I've kinda backed off that stuff. I've got a lot of other irons in the fire, you know?"

"Oh, well, I just remember you telling me about your connections up there. I assume you're still hooked in with the mob, right? You don't get out of that so easily, I guess. Well, this deal, it's big, Dave, and it's a great deal. I know a guy like you could really do well with this."

In one corner of Dave's mind was the party and the pending arrival of his celebrity friend. In another corner was the voice of the hard-learned Pease lesson saying, "Keep it small, keep it manageable." But there was still a small sliver of curiosity. Dave stood up, picked up the base of the phone with its long cord attached and walked out to his sun porch, the music outside growing louder.

"Uh huh. How big we talking? Is it just reefer?"

"No, coke. And we're talking a hundred pounds."

Dave's face went limp. "That's like twenty million on the street, Gary."

"Yeah. That's why my guy is looking for connections to move it. But here's the kicker, this guy got this stuff cheap. We can get it for five mil."

"Gary, I got connections, but that's too much, man. I appreciate you thinking of me, but…"

Gary interrupted, "No, no. You don't need to come up with the whole thing. He's willing to split it up. In fact, he will need to do a smaller deal before going big."

"Who is *he*, Gary?"

"Well, it's more than just a he, but the guy I'm dealing with is named Sanchez. They're moving this stuff up from Nicaragua. I've known this guy for a while, Dave. He's cool. He's cool."

Dave stared blankly out the porch windows. The Chicago skyline was barely noticeable through the hot hazy air. The noise of the party had faded out of his consciousness. The thrill of the deal was starting to overtake him. And then he heard a voice.

"Daddy! Daaaaddddyyyy!" Danny's voice echoing down the hall broke him from his fantasy.

"Gary, now's not a good time. I'm kinda in the middle of a big party, and I got Mr. T coming any minute. I really need to go, man."

"Okay, Dave. But think about it, okay? I could really use your help on this. You enjoy your party, and let's plan to talk in the next couple days. Okay?"

Suddenly Dave felt a pulling on his hand. "Dad, how much longer?"

"Danny, wait downstairs for me. I gotta finish this call, but it should be any time now." Dave tried to not sound annoyed, unsuccessfully.

"I gotta fly, man. Don't count on me. I'll call you if I change my mind. Understand?"

"Okay, Dave, but you really don't want to pass this one up, man. Talk to you soon."

Dave could tell Gary didn't have many other options by how hard he was selling it. His mind was awhirl. If he was going to get into this, he was going to have to take his time and think it through. And thinking it through wasn't about to happen on this day. As he walked out his back door to the yard, the chirping of his beeper signaled it was time. The show was about to start.

Danny peered around the side of the house as the limousine pulled up and parked out front. He saw his uncles move the orange cones blocking the parking place of honor. The long black limo pulled up and sat there, motionless for minutes. Finally, someone emerged. A bald, black man. *Could that be him?* Danny wondered. *Maybe he shaved his Mohawk?* The man walked around to the back of the limo and opened the door. Much to Danny's delight emerged the signature Mr. T. The Mr. T he hoped he'd meet with layers of gold chains around his neck, a white suit coat with no undershirt and long flowing feather earrings. He and his bodyguard greeted Dave with handshakes and hugs, and they strutted to the back yard.

Waiting at the back gate, at the head of the line, stood Danny with his friends and cousins pressing in behind him. Most of the adults respected the celebrity enough to not overwhelm him with hellos or autographs. But the kids couldn't help themselves.

"T," Dave said as they got to the gate, "this is my oldest son, Danny, who I've been telling you about."

"Hey there, Danny," greeted Mr. T. His voice was soft and friendly. A surprise for Danny. "It's nice to meet you. I hear you a big fan of Rocky."

Danny nodded his head energetically.

"Me, too," he said, smiling and shaking Danny's hand. His hand felt rough and calloused as it enveloped Danny's. "Here," T continued, "I brought this picture for you."

Danny grabbed the framed picture with both hands and studied it, mouth agape—a black and white image of Clubber Lang in his boxing attire, his large arms flared out and his gloves perched on his hips. He was jarred from his trance as the crowd moved away from him.

Dave and Mr. T walked around the yard doing introductions, Danny never more than five feet away. Mr. T was friendly and polite, not at all what Danny expected. And he really seemed to love kids. Sensing Danny was his biggest fan there, he gave him some extra attention as they went along.

"So what was your favorite part of the movie, Danny?"

"Uhh, I think the part where you did the…grrrrr." Danny made a fist and did a slow-motion hooking punch through the air with his face all scrunched up and teeth showing.

"Yeah," he laughed. "I called that my monster punch. Had to film it like fifty times or something."

"Hey Mr. T," interjected Danny's Uncle Charlie, "you care to throw a game of horseshoes?" Danny glared at Charlie, but no one noticed. Before he knew it, they were all walking along the chain-link fence to go out behind the yard where the shoe pits were. Danny thought for sure Mr. T and his bodyguard would whoop up on his two uncles, but maybe all the gold threw off his coordination.

Behind the yard was clear sight to Palos Hospital, and before long a string of doctors and nurses had lined up to say hello and request autographs. More people stealing Danny's precious time.

Danny was warned Mr. T wouldn't be able to stay all night, and he felt his time slipping away. Mr. T could sense his energy, so he got down low and sat on the large concrete steps and had a nice long chat with him.

"So Danny, how long you been a fan of Rocky?"

"As long as I can remember. I have 'Rocky II' on tape and watch it all the time."

"Which is your favorite?"

"Oh definitely 'Rocky III'!" he exclaimed with wide eyes and nodding head. "Can you go swimming today?" he hopefully asked.

"Oh man, I would love to. But with all this gold and stuff, it would be hard. I'll come back sometime soon, and you and I can wrestle and go swimming and all that. Okay?" Danny was a little disappointed, but he nodded his head with a smile. Sensing his disappointment, he offered, "How about I sign that picture I brought you? Sound good?" Danny nodded with excitement.

As they continued their conversation, Dave stood off to the side and just took it all in. Scores of people were having fun, listening to music, diving in the pool, laughing and shouting. Danny's eyes glowed as he looked up, smiling at him.

This was Dave's glory. He made this happen. He was the man. People adored him. He brought the smiles to their faces. He brought a smile to Danny's, and that brought a smile to his.

But in a small recess of his mind was the lingering question: *What if?* Could he have his cake and eat it too? As he looked around his yard and surveyed his handiwork, he felt invincible. He'd made it through the arson unscathed. He'd made it through the kidnapping unfettered. He had friends in high places—cops, judges, politicians. Celebrities.

Suddenly, the tension inside him melted away, and he nodded his head in answer to his own silent question.

July 28th, 1982

There was a little voice inside his head warning him. Something didn't feel right. Gary was a little too clingy about this meeting. He must have called him four times since he arrived in Florida to check on where he was and to make sure he'd be to the meeting on time. A small part of Dave knew he should abort, but he reasoned Gary was trying to coordinate a lot of buyers for this load and he just was making sure it all worked out. But just to be safe, he decided to stay back in the hotel and let his friend Jim Sheldon pick up the goods—two pounds of cocaine.

Unfortunately for Dave, the sting was deeper than he predicted. His feeble efforts to avoid its potential couldn't stop it. Jim entered the dingy seaside wharf bar and quickly scanned the mostly empty room. Sitting at the bar were two men. One looked at Jim and nodded. Jim marched over, and made the exchange. Wasting no time, he quickened to the door. For Jim, the party was over.

Back at the hotel, Allmon kept Dave occupied on the phone. But when Dave heard the harsh pounding on the door and telltale warning to open up, he knew his party was over, too. "What did you do, Gary?" he questioned as the door opened and the officers swarmed. The scene unfolded so fast but every detail was seared into his memory.

He heard a cracking sound as the door flew open. The first guy through was short and clad in all black, only the badge affixed to his chest revealing his true identity. He had a helmet on and a thick moustache. He held a shotgun up to his shoulder, and he quickly moved in and to his right. Immediately behind him, another came in with a handgun and headed to Dave's right. Then a third.

"Hands up! On the ground! Face down! Now!"

Dave calmly raised his arms as he felt the second officer wrap his hand around the back of his neck and drag him out of the chair, forcing his face to the ground. The dirty brown carpet burned his cheek from the pressure. *This is overkill. Who were they expecting to find here?*

The weight of the officers' elbows and knees was nothing compared to the pit forming in his stomach. Instant regret filled him, causing a feeling in his chest he hadn't felt since he was nine and his dog got hit by a car. His breathing was erratic, and a tear squeezed out from his painful grimace as the officers cuffed him and lifted him to his feet. The Miranda rights were read to him, but his mind couldn't focus on anything around him. It felt like a surreal dream, like walking through a dense fog. His mind raced with anxiety: Four Seasons. Linda. His mom. Tom Brooks. His dog, Pal. His house. Danny and Dougie.

Unfortunately, his insight came too late. *It's not worth it*, he realized as they ushered him down the hall and to the paddy wagon. *The money is not worth it.*

Little did he comprehend just how true that insight really was.

Chapter Six

THE VOID

1983

Psalm 35:26 – May all who gloat over my distress be put to shame and confusion; may all who exalt themselves over me be clothed with shame and disgrace.

Despite his family's best efforts, Danny found himself adrift without a compass. At first, his mom told him his daddy was just out on a business trip. They expected he'd make bail, but the price tag was set at one million dollars. So they prolonged the ruse. After a couple of weeks, it was that his Uncle Bart suffered a heart attack, and he needed to stay in Florida a little longer. Business trips were common for Dave, and Danny got to talk with him on the phone, but eventually he knew something wasn't quite right about it. Dad was gone. Mom's been away. There were quiet conversations happening all the time. Eventually, they had to tell him their truth. His daddy had been wrongly arrested.

To make the situation worse, so too was Tom Brooks and, eventually, Dave's whole gang. Tom decided to turn on Dave and testify against him, so his family was ushered off to witness protection. It was bad enough to lose his daddy, but Tom's sons were Danny's best friends. Losing everyone at once was disorienting to say the least.

It left a huge void, and voids of this nature don't stay empty for long.

"Miss Lori, I'm going to ride my bike down to the park."

"Which one?" Lori replied. Due to Linda's extensive visits to see friends, family and of course, lawyers, she hired a nanny to help keep an eye on the kids. Lori was a nice, older lady with curly blonde hair and stout body.

"The one by Palos Pool."

"Okay," she said, "but make sure you're home in an hour. I'm making burgers for dinner."

"Got it," he said hurriedly, flying out the door.

The sky was cloudy, and the earlier rains made the bike ride through the fields under the power lines more treacherous than normal. Typically, he'd have some fantasy running through his head as if he was riding a motorcycle or, better yet, flying an X-wing fighter. But his imaginary play would have to wait for the park. He had to keep his eyes trained on the ground lest he find himself over the handlebars with a face full of mud.

The ball fields between the trail and the park were notably quiet. The rain cancelled the games, so concessions were closed and there were very few people to be seen. He rode around to the playground and was pleased it was also empty so he could play some Star Wars without the embarrassment of spying eyes.

After almost an hour, Danny realized he needed to head back. He thought about taking the surface streets home given the soggy ground of the fields, but it was so much farther to go that way. He decided it was worth the risk of a mud streak down his back to save the time and distance. It was a decision he would soon regret.

As he wound his way through the array of ball fields, he spied two kids ahead of him, walking around a large swath of mud and water. One kid was particularly large, much bigger than him. The other was smaller. As he got closer, he recognized the big kid, Brian Felvey.

There's a statistical distribution to physical size no matter your age. Brian was a grade younger, but he was definitely a statistical outlier being bigger than just about everybody in Danny's grade. And Danny, being young for his grade, was small for his.

"Hey kid," the smaller one yelled, "come here."

Danny naïvely aimed his bike in their direction. He didn't sense any danger here. He had no reason to anticipate what was about to happen. "Hey," he exhaled as he pulled up.

"Let me try your bike" the smaller kid ordered. "I want to see if I can make it through this mud."

Danny looked at the deep tire grooves already impressed into the mud and surmised it would be difficult and quite messy. "Ahh, I gotta get home. Sorry." But before he could take off, Brian stepped in front of his bike, straddling his front tire.

"You're going to let him ride it through the mud," he insisted.

"I really gotta go," Danny said as he looked down, averting his eyes. His Spidey senses definitely started tingling. Before he knew it, he and the bike were lying on the ground, his elbow scuffed from the gravel. He looked up at Brian in amazement.

The smaller kid picked up the bike and rode away. Danny stood up and considered running after him, but Brian stopped him.

"Where you going?"

"Give me back my bike!" Danny yelled, straining to get away from Brian's grasp. He felt helpless. Soon, the smaller kid turned around and took a hard run at the mud. He flew through, spraying mud all over himself and the bike and yelling with delight. Brian's fat face erupted with a grin.

"I'm gonna tell the cops," yelled Danny, grasping at anything he could think of to end this nightmare.

Brian's face turned to a scowl, and he looked down at Danny. "You ain't gonna tell no one about anything! You know what you're gonna do? You're gonna take off that Cubs hat and throw it in the mud."

Danny hesitated, processing Brian's demand. Slowly, he took off the hat and looked at it. It was the hat his dad had bought him a few years prior when they went to Wrigley Field and got to go up and meet Jack Brickhouse. He threw it down as softly as he could, figuring he'd do what he had to in order to make this end. Brian lifted his giant foot and stomped it into the mud as the two bullies laughed, and Danny held back his tears.

But Brian wasn't done. "Now, sit in the mud," he ordered calmly but firmly. Danny shook his head. "Sit in it or I'll squash you in it!" he demanded with more force.

Danny considered his options. Should he run? No, they'd still have his bike. Should he fight? Brian would crush him. So, he did the only thing he felt he could do. He slowly stepped over and his feet sank in the mud, which oozed up around his shoes. He stood there looking at his feet when he heard, "Sit!" He gradually lowered himself into the mud and started to cry.

"Ohhh, baby's gonna cry," the smaller kid chided as they laughed. Brian was readying to bark another order of humiliation at Danny when a voice in the distance ended the scene.

"Hey!" the man yelled, "What's going on?"

The smaller kid dropped Danny's bike, and they high-tailed it out of there. Danny stood up and tried to lift his feet from the mud. He got his left foot out, but when he pulled the right one, the shoe remained behind. The man walked up and put his hand on Danny's shoulder.

"Kid, you okay?"

Danny nodded through teary eyes. "My shoe is stuck."

The man reached over and lifted the muddy shoe from the pit. "Do you know those kids?" Danny shrugged his shoulders. "You shouldn't let them do that to you, kid. Stand up for yourself." Danny nodded and carefully slipped his foot back in the shoe. He didn't even try to unearth his Cubs hat. He walked over, picked up his bike and thanked the guy for helping him out.

The ride home helped him to compose his emotions and concoct an "accidental fall" story, but it did little to help him with his feelings of weakness and shame. He wished so badly his daddy was home or at least his mommy. He ditched his shoes and his bike in the garage, took a shower, and laid awake that night, dreading the next day at school.

The playground is a tough place sometimes, even at school with recess monitors. In a fitting twist of fate, Danny had been a bit of a bully himself back in the first grade. His Napoleon complex had found legs, and he'd go around pushing and punching other kids. That is, until they started fighting back. One day, he had picked a fight with a kid, who quickly dispatched Danny through a series of breath-stealing upper cuts. That would be the last time Danny fought, or wanted to fight. Humiliation brought humility and civility.

But now, in the fifth grade, humiliation brought fear. Danny carefully avoided Brian the next day. Then the next. Weeks went by and eventually Danny started to play on the swings and run around without looking over his shoulder all the time. He began to believe that Brian wouldn't dare do anything violent at school. Wrong again, Danny.

It felt like a normal recess. The athletes were out in the field playing kick ball or shooting hoops on the court. The girls swarmed the jungle gym and played hopscotch. Everyone else gathered in groups of two or three and just played tag or swung on the swings.

That's where Danny was when Brian reentered the scene. Danny and his friend Mike were seeing who could jump farthest off the swings when he saw Brian's enormous shadow approaching. He decided the best strategy was to play ostrich, just keep swinging, look toward Mike, and pray Brian would just pass by.

"Hey dork. Hey dork! You're on my swing!"

"These aren't your swings," Mike retorted. Danny was astounded. Did he know who he was talking back to?

"Shut up, I ain't talking to you anyway."

Danny stuck to his strategy and kept swinging when he felt the pull on the chain, launching him awkwardly to the ground. He looked around to see if he could find a recess monitor. *Where's Mrs. Robinson when you need her?*

Mike got off his swing and shouted some insults at Brian, but he retreated like a scared cat once Brian flashed a little anger his way. Suddenly, however, the whole scene changed.

Unbeknownst to Danny, over on the slide, Rich Kuduk watched the commotion unfold. Rich was a big, muscular kid. A loner. A bit of an outcast. He sometimes came to school unkempt and got made fun of, behind his back, for having BO. But as Rich entered the picture, Danny only saw a hero.

Rich charged over to Brian and grabbed the swing, stopping it. "You're a real tough guy, huh?" Rich yelled. The look on Brian's face brought a smile to Danny's. Rich grabbed his shirt with his left hand and pulled him off the swing. With his right fist raised, he threatened, "You like to pick on smaller guys, do ya?"

"No! No!" Brian replied in terror. Brian was bigger than Rich but not nearly as strong, and you'd have thought it was his father scolding him by his reaction.

"Apologize to him!"

"I'm sorry," Brian apologized in desperate fashion.

"Tell him you'll never pick on him again!"

"I'll never pick on you again! I promise."

"If you do, then you'll be dealing with me!" Rich shoved Brian away, letting go of his shirt.

Brian never picked on Danny again. Humiliation brought civility.

And Danny found himself a new best friend.

Chapter Seven

ACTING OUT

1983

Jeremiah 32:18 - You show love to thousands but bring the punishment for the parents' sins into the laps of their children after them.

    Danny's eyes bugged out of his head as Rich lifted the twenty pound dumbbell and curled it with one arm as if it were a balloon. Rich had a cocky smirk on his face as he pumped the weight, gloating over Danny's silly challenge. Earlier that day, Danny struggled to lift it with both arms, arching his back with a form that should have slipped a disc. He knew Rich was strong, but he figured this would challenge even him.

    Rich set the dumbbell down and when he stood back up his eyes noticed something he hadn't seen in all his visits to Danny's house before. "What's in that locked cabinet?" he asked.

    Above Danny's fridge were typical narrow cabinet doors. Typical except for the tiny black plastic lock and gold-plated clasp holding them shut. Danny hadn't thought about those cabinets in quite some time, despite their being in plain sight every day. That cabinet is where his dad, upon return home from work each day, placed his handgun for safe keeping.

"My dad used to keep his guns up there," Danny answered as Rich gave him a look of intrigue.

"What kind of guns?" he asked. Danny just shrugged his shoulders. "You know where the key is?"

"Nuh uh," Danny answered with a shake of his head.

Rich stood in front of the fridge, surveying the lock. "I think we can pick it," he said as he looked down upon Danny, expecting a nod of approval.

Rich's influence on Danny had grown since the playground rescue months before. It turned out the socially awkward hulk was pretty awesome. He and Danny shared many of the same interests, like WWF wrestling and weapons. But where Danny would pretend to shoot, Rich actually had pellet guns. He actually had knives. He actually had shot a shotgun before. Danny would pretend his bike was a motorcycle. Rich had a motor bike—at eleven! So when Rich suggested something, Danny always went along. One time, he even dared Danny to expose himself in front of his aunt and grandmother. He did it. So it was with little hesitation that Danny agreed to help open the cabinet.

He glanced downstairs to see his babysitter sitting and watching TV. He slowly and quietly pulled the pocket door closed. Then Rich jumped up on the countertop to take a closer look.

"All we need is a screwdriver," he said in a loud whisper. "A small one. Phillips."

Danny ran out to the garage and returned in a flash, handing the black and yellow handle to his friend. Rich studied the clasp and began to twist the three tiny screws. In a minute, the doors were open. And Rich's face lit up.

"Holy s#it!" he whisper yelled as he stood and stared, mouth agape. Danny had pulled over a kitchen chair to get a better view, his heart racing at the speed of sound. Peering into the cabinet, he saw some rectangular cardboard boxes labeled as ammunition. To the right, he could see the wood grain and black handles of the guns, sheathed in their holsters. Rich reached in and pulled one out.

"A snub-nosed thirty-eight," he said, removing it from its case. Danny stared with wide eyes of disbelief. *Are we really doing this? And how does Rich know what kind of gun that is?* He turned his attention to the basement, softly hopping off his chair to peer through the crack in the door. No signs of life. But Danny's adrenaline overpowered his admiration.

"We gotta close it up," he rasped with a hiss. Rich put the gun back and quietly closed the door, softly leaping from the counter and taking a seat. Even the cool Rich Kuduk breathed heavy from the excitement.

"Is she coming?" he asked.

"It sounded like it. Lock it up."

Rich jumped back up and put the screws back in. Their morsel of excitement was over. For now.

Danny loved the adrenaline rush of breaking the rules. This little lock-picking escapade was certainly not his first experience. Probably unsurprisingly, he first learned the trade from his daddy.

Many years prior, Dave and Danny were on a road trip to visit Linda's parents in North Carolina. As they got close, they stopped to have dinner with one of Dave's friends. Apparently time got away from Dave as they were supposed to pick up Linda and baby Dougie from the airport, but they found themselves late for the arrival. When Dave noticed the page from Linda, he hurriedly paid the bill and rushed out. On the drive to get them, Dave admonished Danny, "Don't tell your mom about our stop for dinner, all right?"

"Why not?" he asked innocently.

"She might get mad because we're late to get her. If she asks, we've just been driving the whole time. Okay?"

Danny agreed. But unfortunately for Dave, his son's neophyte skills of deceit couldn't restrain his urge to reveal the truth. After he blurted it out some number of hours later, he regretted the tension and chaos it created between his parents. *It would have been better to keep the secret*, he thought. It was the first callousing of his conscience.

From there, Danny's temptation turned to the shiny marbles and packs of gum at the Ben Franklin drug store down the street. It was so easy to buy something small, get it bagged up, then walk out through the back door of the store, picking up free treasures along the way. Danny must have done it a dozen times. Then he got sloppy.

One day, he was eyeing a small red squirt gun. As he held it in his hand, he felt the pull. He didn't have any money to buy anything that day. His shorts had no pockets. He stood there and contemplated. He looked to his right, toward the back door. All clear. He looked to his left. The old store manager was walking around. Danny waited. Finally, he shoved the gun down his shorts and briskly walked out, the bell on the back door clanging as it slammed behind him. He hurriedly fumbled to lift his bike and saw something from the corner of his eye. The store manager was peering out the window. A chill ran down his back.

The old man opened the door and came out. "You okay, son? Let me help you with that bicycle," he offered, grabbing the banana seat and helping Danny lift it up. "Nice bike," he offered with a smile.

"Thanks," Danny said, trying to avoid eye contact and hoping he didn't know about the gun.

"So, I guess you really like that squirt gun, huh?" he asked. "Can I have it back?"

Danny looked down in dread. He reached into his shorts and handed over his loot. He didn't say a word.

"Now, son, taking things like this is wrong. You know that?"

Danny nodded his head. His eyes carried the gloss of guilt in them.

"What do you think I should do here, son, call the police?"

Danny shook his head violently, his eyes widening. "Please don't. I'm sorry. I'll never do it again."

The old man pondered for a few seconds. "Okay, I won't do that. But I want you to go home and tell your folks what you did. Will you promise to tell them?"

Danny knew what he needed to say. "Yes, sir," making eye contact for the first time.

"Okay. You go along home then and tell them."

Danny never rode his bike so fast in all his life, then or since. As the dread gave way to elation, he couldn't believe he got away with it. For the normal boy, this would serve to curtail future nefarious ambitions. And it did cause Danny to avoid the Ben Franklin for a while. But the lesson he learned was not that crime doesn't pay. The lesson he learned was that people are dopes. They can be manipulated. If people think you're a nice kid, you can get away scotch free.

So Danny honed his nice-kid skills, and he continued to test the boundaries of what he could get away with. But this gun escapade with Rich would turn out to be like advanced calculus to a ten-year-old.

Rich called Danny later that night. "We gotta get those guns out of the cabinet. Then we can play with them without risking getting caught. Can you pop the clasp like I did?"

"I think so," Danny replied. "But what do I say if I get caught?"

"Just say you noticed the screws were loose and you're just fixing it."

Sounded logical, to a ten-year-old. That night, Danny played a careful game. Lori was staying overnight as his mother was off dealing with who knows what. He waited for her to take her usual spot in front of the TV in their living room after dinner. The room was adjacent to but out of sight of the kitchen. He then quietly climbed up on the counter and began to twist the tiny gold screws, one by one. At one point, he heard Lori stirring.

"What were you doing up there?" she asked after hearing Danny jump down from the counter.

"Uh, I was just trying to get a bowl off the top shelf."

"Which one? I'll grab it."

That was close. Too close. If Lori had looked just twelve inches to her right, she would have seen the missing screws and the screwdriver on the top of the fridge. It's a shame she didn't. But she was short enough and apparently distracted enough not to notice.

Danny ran upstairs and called Rich. "Dude, I almost got caught! I can't get them down with her here."

"Well, I guess if you're too chicken, then we'll have to figure out another plan." Danny could hear the disappointment in his voice. He couldn't bear it.

"I'll try again. But if I get caught, I'll be grounded for weeks."

Truth is Danny had been grounded many times. Normally it didn't really scare him because the infractions were minor and the punishments never persisted. But he knew this was a different level. Regardless, he pushed through his fear and eventually liberated two guns and two cartons of ammo, hiding them away in the piles of boxes and clothes stored in his mom's bedroom sun porch. He was careful to put the screws back in place and make sure nothing looked amiss. He called Rich, excited and proud.

The next morning, Rich came over and they holed up on the sun porch like two hostage takers. Danny held the snub-nose thirty-eight, its contours and form being more familiar to him. But what surprised him was the weight. It was much heavier than his toy guns. He pulled the trigger; that was much harder too.

Meanwhile, Rich played around with the other gun, the automatic. This gun was less familiar and much more intimidating to Danny. Rich handled it like it was second nature, popping out the ammo clip and emptying it. Then he pulled back the slide to eject the chambered load. He pulled the trigger and showed Danny how everything worked. Despite his tutelage, Danny remained intimidated.

After messing around with them for an hour or so, Rich went home and Danny's life went back to boredom. Normally he entertained himself quite well. It wasn't hard to do with a huge yard, pool, pets, toys galore and a VCR. But they felt pale as earthshine after the surges of adrenaline he had felt over the past couple days. And he couldn't resist the allure. He snuck back up to the sun porch to get his fix.

Holding the shiny thirty-eight, he aimed it out the row of windows at the cars driving in and out of the hospital. CLICK! He imagined shooting them and the loud bang it would make. He imagined bullet holes erupting to explosions as his imaginary villains tried to escape. Nothing gory or deadly. More like the "A-Team" and other 80's TV shows. A kind of sanitized violence.

But even the thirty-eight didn't give Danny the fix he wanted. The automatic called to him. With fluttering breath, he reached his tiny arm over the clothes obscuring their hiding spot. He dug around and felt the steely weapon, holding it up close to his face. He looked at it like he was studying for a test or something. He found the lever Rich showed him that ejected the clip. He pressed it, and the clip fell out. It was full of bullets. He pushed with his thumb to remove a bullet, but he found it harder than he expected. It took two thumbs. One by one, he emptied the magazine and put the clip back in.

He wanted to pull the trigger, but he remembered Rich told him there could still be a bullet in the chamber. He tried to pull the slide back, but he wasn't strong enough. Turning the gun toward his face, he closed his left eye and stared down the barrel, moving it around to try to shine some light down there. Darkness. He put the barrel up to his mouth. Wrapping his lips around the barrel, he blew as hard as he could. Air moved through the barrel. It seemed there was no bullet in there.

He sauntered to the windows, his hands wet and shaking, and looked out at the cars. With two hands, he held the gun and aimed. He put his right index finger on the trigger and closed his left eye to line up the sights. A mother with her little girl got into their grey Chevy Nova. She started the car, and the brake lights came on. Danny lined up the gun's sights on the rear window as the car backed out of the spot. She turned back to the right and swung around so now Danny had a clear sight of her head. He took aim...

"Bang!" he yelled in his high-pitched voice. He was pretty sure there was nothing in there, but he was too scared to pull the trigger. Still, he really wanted to. He deliberated for a minute or so, then walked over to the balcony door. He reached up and slid the upper slide lock out. The lower slide lock was stuck. He put the gun down and used two hands, springing it out of its tunnel, and gravity opened the door.

Danny picked the gun back up and looked out over the pool to the hospital. He stepped back in to the porch and looked into his parents' room and down the hall. The coast was clear. Back on the balcony, he took a deep breath. He held the gun above his head, aiming it up into the air while covering his head and both his ears with his left arm. Holding his breath and squeezing his eyes shut, he began to apply pressure to the trigger. It didn't move. His heart couldn't take the anticipation, so he squeezed as hard as he could...

BANG! The sound echoed off the hospital and reverberated for two or three seconds. Danny dropped the gun, his right hand vibrated, and his mind went to chaos. The gun looked like it was broken, the slide remained back, showing it was out of ammo. Danny's ears rang. He had never heard something so loud, not even his Uncle Mark's M80.

The first thing occurring to him was that Lori must have heard. Danny picked up the gun and quickly stashed it away. He ran down the stairs and looked for Lori. His heartbeat was still at max.

"Lori? Did you hear that noise?" he asked with fluttered voice.

"What noise?" she said. He couldn't believe she didn't hear anything.

"I thought I heard an explosion."

"No, I didn't hear anything like that."

Relief started to settle in. He ran back upstairs to the porch and to the balcony. On the ground was a shell casing for the bullet. He picked it up and looked out to his yard. Then his relief turned to panic. *Heidi!*

He knew his dog wasn't in the yard so he ran downstairs. The laundry room door was open, so she wasn't inside either. That could mean only one thing. Heidi was out roaming the neighborhood again. Terror consumed Danny. What if the bullet came down on her? Don't tell a ten-year-old who's just experienced emotional trauma about the statistical odds of a bullet randomly coming down coincidentally where his dog just happened to be standing. Rationality is nowhere to be found in situations like this.

Danny ran out of the house and tore through his neighbors' backyards like he was being chased by bees. As loud as his little lungs could muster, he yelled "Heeeeeiiiidddddiiiii!" With each step and each yell, his fears became more acute. If she was hurt, he would never forgive himself. *Why did I do that?* he thought as regret filled his heart. *I should have been more careful.*

Finally, like a scene from a Lassie movie, Heidi emerged from some brush and ran toward Danny full tilt. Relief overcame him as he fell down and hugged her coarse dark fur, her tongue licking his sweaty face. You could almost hear the triumphant music playing, like the happy ending to a cheesy movie.

Only, this happiness wouldn't last for long.

It was a warm, serene spring day for Danny, walking home from school through the backyards and powerline fields of Palos. For the first time in weeks, he felt normal, like he had skirted certain doom. He walked along with two sticks, one in each hand, and had them battle each other in light-saber fashion. This was a common game for Danny. A way to pass the time on the long, repetitive walk. One stick would eventually win the battle as the other one broke. So then he would find another contender and repeat the battle.

He walked down 123rd Place toward his house. Passing by the Sonic's, the Thompson's, eventually arriving at his driveway. He took two steps onto the pavement when the kitchen door opened and his mom popped out. It was very unusual for her to pre-greet him in the driveway, and the look on her face was serious. His heartbeat stuttered; he believed he was a goner.

"Grab those garbage cans behind you," she directed in a stern voice. Danny did an about face and dragged the cans slowly up to the garage. *Okay*, he hoped, *maybe that was just a false alarm.* He deposited the cans next to the garage and said a silent prayer in his mind.

"Have a seat," she said through gritted teeth as he entered the door. She was already seated in her usual spot with an unmistakably serious look on her face. "So, were you ever going to tell me?"

"Tell you what?" he asked, still hoping this was a false alarm. Truth is, there were many infractions she could have been talking about.

"YOU TOOK GOD D@MN GUNS OUT OF THIS HOUSE!" The words seemed louder to Danny than the gunshot. And they would echo in his soul for the rest of his life.

After telling Rich about the shooting, Rich suggested taking the guns over to his place. They would be safer there, he claimed, less likely to be found. Danny was happy to oblige and get the evidence out of sight. But within a week, Rich called Danny and told him the bad news—his older brother John found the guns. He was debating what to do about it. Danny desperately tried to negotiate with John through Rich, but he feared his ship was sunk.

In the following days, the situation gave Danny a true psychosomatic reaction. His stomach literally began to ache as the threat of reprisal was upon him. It was so bad that his mom mistook his retching sobs as being related to his father's arrest and absence, even though Danny denied it. Regardless, she went out and signed him up for counseling sessions.

As days stacked up, Danny began to relax a little. Maybe Rich's brother wouldn't rat them out. It had been almost two weeks. Maybe he'd just keep the guns for himself instead. His mom's deafening declaration had answered that question.

Through fluttered breath and teary eyes, Danny explained how they had picked the lock, hid the guns and eventually moved them to Rich's. In trying to save his skin, he twisted the story so that Rich sounded like the bad guy—like he was just along for the ride. And he never dared to admit to the shooting.

As hard as it was for Danny to sit there and admit his transgressions with his mom, it was even harder for him to admit them to his daddy, who called right as they were ending the interrogation. Linda handed the phone to Danny. "You tell him," she said. To his surprise, Dave didn't scold him. He just asked questions in a serious tone and told Danny to give the phone back to his mom.

Suffice to say Danny's life changed that day. For one, it taught Danny there are limits to how far he can push his misdeeds. There was a line somewhere where he could keep things secret and in control. He would spend the rest of his pre-teen and teenage years trying to find this line.

Also, no longer would Rich Kuduk be such an unfettered influence in his life. They would still see each other at school and a few years later they would reunite for a while and carry on a new chapter of mischief. But for the most part, Danny would have to find other ways to shore up his fragile ego. And unfortunately, he would turn in every direction except the one way he really needed to.

Chapter Eight

LOSING FAITH

October 1984

Job 6:8 – Oh that I might have my request, that God would grant me the thing that I long for!

Children are born with an inherent optimism. They crawl around on the floor, looking at people around them who are upright and walking, and they believe they can do that. They try to stand, and their large heads and wobbly legs result in their first set-back. But they persist. Up and down, they are encouraged by their caretakers, so they never give up. They improve and see positive results. Little by little, they stabilize. They take steps. Before you know it, they're running through the house like wild animals.

The same process happens for a child's ability to see and trust in God's work in their lives. But whereas everyone around them walks and the feedback is immediate and tangible, the same cannot be said of faith. Those around Danny were not pointing out how God might be working. They were not encouraging him to seek and trust. Nevertheless, Danny picked up enough through osmosis to believe in God and to know to pray. And through all the developments of the past two years, Danny knew he needed to pray to God. Unfortunately, however, he was never taught the true purpose of prayer. And his childish understanding was about to challenge whatever optimism he had left.

Linda stood outside of Danny's door, scared to death to knock, terrified to go in. She just stood there in her robe, looking at the handmade poster board hung on the door, trying to come up another excuse to delay. Or at least with a different way of telling him the bad news, a way that would minimize the pain.

Dave's trial for murder, conspiracy and kidnapping had ended the week prior and the jury finally returned their verdict—on Danny's birthday of all days. With all the uncertainty and chaos, the family decided to distract and shelter him from the stress as best they could. No sense in giving him pieces of bad news until the whole drama unfolded and his sentencing was passed. And no point in ruining his birthday, they reasoned.

His birthday party the day before was supposed to be a fun distraction. They arranged to have some family and Danny's friends over to swim and play at his grandparents'. What could be more exciting in October than to slide, dive and splash away in warmth? Danny put out invitations to six of his school friends and was quite excited to show off his Taj Mahal. But the news of the conviction and sentencing broke and most of his friends canceled at the last hour. Unaware of the reason, Danny felt like he had no friends, and Linda's heart broke for him.

Still, they were able to salvage some fun with his cousins and the couple of friends who did come, and they were successful in keeping Danny insulated from the bad news. But time finally ran out. No more deception. No more delays.

Just do it already, she admonished herself. *Don't beat around the bush. Tear the bandage off.* Linda reached down to the shiny gold knob and held it. *Why do I have to be the one again? That b@stard should be the one doing this!* She twisted the knob, revealing Danny, curled up in the fetal position facing her. His eyes opened, and he stretched out with a big yawn.

"Danny," she murmured as she walked to him. "It's time to wake up." She sat down on the bed and put her hand on his legs, gently rubbing.

"Uhh, what time is it?"

"It's nine thirty. Listen, Danny, I have to tell you something. Your dad's verdict came in."

Danny stopped rubbing his eyes and looked at his mom's. He could tell by the look on her face. "I don't want to hear it," he said, pulling the covers over his head.

"You have to hear this. You can't run away from it," she admonished, pulling the covers off his head. "Your dad was found guilty. He's been given life in prison."

Life in prison. Danny didn't hear anything else past that. He had no idea that was even a possibility. They talked for a few more minutes before Linda got up and left the room, closing the door and leaving Danny to lie there, alone. And he never felt more alone. The prayer he offered while at his Grandparent's church a few weeks back had failed. Again.

He turned onto his side and looked over at the poster of Mr. Spock from "Star Trek" hanging on his closet door. *I wish I was an emotionless alien like him. Purely rational.*

He shook his head and his eyes wandered over to the silver crucifix hanging above his door—a fixture which had been there since he was a baby. He sat up and walked over, stretching up on his tippy-toes, to take it down. He studied the image of the little boy overlaid on the cross, kneeling, praying with his eyes closed. He pitied that naive child. What a fool. He reached to his right and opened a dresser drawer. The heavy metal cross clanged loudly as he dropped it on the toy cars and trinkets held within. *Never again*, he vowed, slamming it shut before heading back to his bed.

He felt like staying wrapped up in his gentle covers all day. *Why get up? What's the point?*

In her bedroom right next to Danny's, Linda just stood there, her eyes squeezed shut and sobs of pain overtaking her. She was paralyzed with a terrifying thought. It was a notion that had circled her subconscious ever since she got that call two years before, but she never allowed it to surface. She kept it down and forced herself to keep moving forward. But now, it overwhelmed her: *How am I going to keep this family from falling apart?*

Chapter Nine

ADAPTING

1985

Matthew 13:15 – For this people's heart has become calloused; they hardly hear with their ears, and they have closed their eyes. Otherwise they might see with their eyes, hear with their ears, understand with their hearts and turn, and I would heal them.

"What's the difference between ignorance and apathy?" Todd asked Danny as they rolled along on their way home from school. Danny looked up for a second, then shrugged his shoulders. "I don't know, and I don't care!" John's eyes widened like he was so clever.

"Ha ha," Danny said, deadpan. "Hey, I thought I'd tell you a good time travel joke. But you didn't like it!"

Todd busted out in laughter, exposing his silver braces. "Good one!"

The school bus is a lot like the playground—they're both more fun when you're in the oldest grade. In seventh grade, Danny mostly sat by himself and daydreamed. Now in eighth, he was much more comfortable socializing with his bus-mates.

"See you in the morning," Danny said as he darted down the narrow aisle and hopped down the stairs. He threw a wave at everyone as the door squealed closed and the bus grumbled off.

The walk from one end of 123rd Place to the other wasn't very long, but the cold wind quickened Danny's normal pace. At the mid-point, right before the power-line fields, he glanced over at the house of his old best friends, Tommy and Jimmy Brooks. He'd spent so many hours there in years past. But they were whisked away and hidden as a part of a witness protection program. Now it was occupied by a new family, the Trusses. They had two kids just like the Brooks family, same ages even, one older and one younger than Danny. His mom had encouraged him to stop in and introduce himself, but Danny was too intimidated for that.

A short five minutes later, he walked into his kitchen, where he was greeted by his mom. "How was school?"

"Fine. You're not at work?"

"I'm going with to visit your dad tonight. Let Heidi in please, then we gotta hit the road."

Danny grimaced and set his backpack on the floor. He thought about the partially built Starship Enterprise up in his bedroom and slowly stomped down the stairs to let his dog in. Legos would have to wait.

It had been a couple of weeks since they'd made the trek downtown to visit. Dave was extradited to Chicago under the pretense of charges for the arson of the store on Roseland many years prior. In reality, it was a ruse to bring Dave up to see if he'd squeal on his supposed mob connections. And while he knew quite a bit and the concept of having the government help him instead of hurt him was appealing, he was also smart enough to know to keep quiet. Still, he was able to prolong the situation for nine months until they finally figured out he wasn't going to squeal. So the arson trial finally commenced; hence the hiatus in visits for the past couple of weeks.

After letting the dog in, Danny ran up to his room to feed his hamster and grab his Walkman. If he was going to be trapped, at least he could listen to his own radio station. He sank into the plush blue seats of the Continental next to his brother and dialed in the top-forty radio station, drowning out the twangy music his mom insisted on torturing them with. They made a quick stop to pick up Grandma Alice, then they hit I-55 headed downtown. At least they were headed in the right direction for that time of day; most traffic was headed the other way. There were rare occasions where an accident might double the forty-five minute jaunt and cut into their visiting time. But this day, it moved smoothly. Danny passed the time with music and daydreams, envisioning himself flying alongside the car in a winged jet pack, weaving around the street lights with agility and control.

In seemingly no time, they pulled into the parking lot adjacent to the Metropolitan Correctional Center. The tall, wedge-shaped building and its concrete exterior was a stark contrast to the typical buildings surrounding it. Many of the tall narrow windows were lit up with the silhouettes of inmates gazing upon the city, having daydreams of their own.

They entered through the heavy glass door, and Danny, Dougie and Alice sat on the hard plastic chairs while Linda walked up to the uniformed receptionist to check in. They were there early, so the boring drive gave way to the boring wait. Danny got up and walked around the glass-walled lobby, looking around at the diverse set of people waiting with them. Dougie was much younger and hadn't been exposed to as much diversity, so he tended to stay close to Mom or Grandma. But Danny's experience working at the auto-parts store gave him some confidence in being around poorer-looking people and minorities.

He was proud of his ability to act comfortably in intimidating environments. To him, it was the ultimate sign of strength. A strength his dad displayed during their visits, always cool and confident while interacting with his fellow inmates. Danny's mind wandered back to his recurring fantasy of living there, in prison, with his dad. He mentored Danny, showing him the ropes—how to handle dangerous inmates or bribe the guards in order to get special treats in. It seemed to him to be such a simple and attractive existence—no school, no worries about the future. His naïve fantasies kept him from truly feeling for his dad's plight. A convenient defense mechanism for someone training to be a logical Vulcan.

After fifteen minutes, they finally got the call as "Domberg!" echoed in the triangular room. They filed over, got searched and rode up to the fourteenth floor where they ushered in to the visiting room, taking one of their usual spots at a round table near the back wall of the brightly lit, triangular room. The room was abuzz with conversation as loved ones caught up. About half of the dozen or so tables were filled. There were two guards in the room, and two more seated behind a large window. Danny wondered why the guards were always so portly, like it was a job requirement or something.

While they waited for Dave, Alice took out two decks of cards, a visitation tradition. She pushed one across the table to Danny and dealt herself a game of solitaire.

Danny spied his brother picking his nose. "You digging for treasure in there?" The seven-year-old feigned flicking a booger in his direction. Danny dodged the imaginary projectile and slugged Dougie on the arm. Linda quickly quashed the burgeoning spat. "Danny, keep your hands to yourself!" She wiped Dougie's finger with a napkin from her purse. He noticed she seemed particularly uptight this evening, but it didn't register why that might be.

"He flicked a booger at me!" he protested.

"Enough," she replied through gritted teeth.

The buzzing sound of the inmate door signaled Dave's arrival. Danny and Dougie sprang from their chairs as if the buzzing sound was an electric shock, and they raced each other to get the first hug. As usual, Dave just grabbed them both in a group-hug.

"Hey kiddos," he said through his smile. The embrace broke, and he looked Danny up and down. "Man, I think you grew another inch in the last two weeks."

"Dad, did you see the 'Rocky IV' commercial?" Danny asked excitedly. It obviously didn't dawn on him that Dave didn't get to watch much TV.

"No," Dave replied, with his eyebrows raised and forehead wrinkled.

"Apollo dies!" he declared, as if the character were a real person. "The Russian kills him in a fight!"

"No way!"

"Rocky's gonna kick his butt," Dougie interjected, vying for Dave's attention.

"He better. We can't have those Russians ruining the movie, can we?"

"I don't know, Dad," Danny shook his head, "the guy is six foot six!"

"Always remember, it's not about how big you are. It's about how smart you are. Speaking of which, you gonna make the honor roll again?"

"Yeah, I think so," replied Danny as they arrived back at the table.

"Yeah, but no water beds this time. Right, Dave?" Linda's eyes burned a hole through Dave's. Dave had promised Danny a water bed if he made honor roll for the first time at the end of seventh grade. Linda obviously didn't like him writing checks that she had to cash.

"I love my water bed. Keeps me cool in the summer and warm in the winter."

Dave leaned over and gave his mom a kiss and took a seat. He didn't give one to Linda but the kids were oblivious. Instead, they instinctively asked for money for the vending machines. Alice pulled five ones from her purse and handed them to Dave. Dave handed them to Danny and said, "You two go and get what you want and bring me an Almond Joy, okay?" It was unusual for Dave to not go with them. But the lure of sugar overwhelmed any concern about it.

As they stared at the array of chips and candy, Dave looked over to Linda. "You ready for this?"

"Uh huh," she nodded her head with a look of satisfaction. "You get to do this one. Not me for once."

"Oh geez," Alice interjected, "are you going to tell them right away? Maybe I should go to the bathroom."

"I'd just as soon get it over with," Dave replied. Alice got up and left.

The boys returned to their seats, and Danny opened up the deck of cards preparing for a match, singing a song he listened to on the way in under breath.

"What's that song you're singing?" Dave asked him.

"It's called 'Take On Me' by A-Ha." Danny sang a couple of lines more audibly.

"Hmm, sounds like a real winner. Look, guys, your mom and I have something we need to tell you." Dougie gnawed on his Crunch bar, and Danny continued to shuffle. "Guys," Dave repeated, trying to get their attention. "Your mom and I had to make a tough decision recently. With all my legal troubles, in order to keep the government from taking Four Seasons, we've decided to get a divorce." Danny looked up from the cards. "It doesn't mean we don't love you. But your mom now owns Four Seasons, so it's protected. You understand?"

A year ago, this news might have stunned or shocked Danny like the news of his conviction. Danny just nodded his head and went back to shuffling.

"Does this mean you aren't ever coming home?" Dougie asked.

"Well," Dave replied slowly, "once I get a retrial and get my illegal sentencing overturned, we'll see about all of that. In the meantime, just know this changes nothing about how I feel about your or your mom. Okay?"

Dougie went back to gnawing, and Danny started dealing a game of gin rummy. Linda looked over to Dave and shook her head. The reason for the divorce was a nice ploy because it was partially true. The full truth was that Linda felt relief to have an out. The pain of betrayal had taken its toll. The old feeling was gone. Now when she looked at him, all she felt was anger.

"So Dad," Danny broke the awkward silence, "what's your favorite meal here?"

Dave and Linda didn't expect such an abrupt transition. They imagined there would be questions or crying or whatever. Linda considered forcing the conversation to continue, but before she could settle on it, Dave began to answer.

"Well, most of the food is quite bland. But I'd say the chicken is pretty good once you put some salt on it. Especially if it comes with some gravy."

"How about drinks? Do you get Cokes or something?"

"We can buy those. Otherwise we get coffee or tea or water. Or milk, but I never drink that."

"Do you have a job here," Dougie asked.

"Inmates can get jobs. When I was in Florida, I basically ran the mailroom. Guards there were morons. But I haven't had the spare time to pursue anything up here."

Alice returned gingerly approaching the table to make sure everything was calm. She sat down and continued her game, chatting with Linda while the boys tended to their own rituals.

Just like always, the visit went by too quickly for Dave, as they stood up for goodbye hugs and kisses. What was more painful than usual for this goodbye is he knew his time in Chicago was coming to an end. He wanted so badly to stay there, to slow the march of time and enjoy his boys for another month. Another week. Another day. But the worst part of Dave's punishment wasn't the bad food. It wasn't the constant threat of violence. It wasn't even the divorce. It was the distance. The distance it put between him and his parents. The distance it put between him and his boys.

It definitely wasn't worth it.

Chapter Ten

THE NEW NORMAL

1987

Job 6:11 – What strength do I have, that I should still hope? What prospects, that I should be patient?

It's amazing how engrossing counting can be when you have little else to do. Dave was always successful in part because he was pretty good at counting—money, auto parts, cards. Now he found himself counting different things, although for similarly selfish reasons—cigarettes, favors, days.

Sitting in his plain beige cell, he scratched out the number of days served and his "good time" each month since being arrested. He wrote on anything he could find, napkins, folders, scraps of yellow paper. He was having an impossible time reconciling his time served compared to the state's records. *Shouldn't be this hard to count up five years of time*, he lamented.

A life sentence, you see, isn't really a life sentence. And Dave didn't have one life sentence anyway; he had two, thirty years each to be served consecutively for conspiracy to commit murder and racketeering. Plus another fifty years for orchestrating the Pease kidnapping. The prosecution painted Dave as the self-declared ring leader for a drug-smuggling syndicate. As such, all crimes committed by the members of that syndicate were his responsibility. According to them, Dave ordered Pease to be killed. And since most of his cronies turned on and testified against him for reduced charges, there were many voices against his one.

Dave felt a warm breeze on the back of his neck. "Would you please stop blowing your smoke on me, Ricky?" He insisted in a stern and annoyed voice, not turning his head.

"Sorry, man, bad habit," His short, portly cellmate replied.

Dave didn't much care for Ricky, but he was better than the previous couple. Save for some bad habits, like occasionally blowing his smoke really hard and snoring, he wasn't that bad. And besides, he didn't have enough cigarettes to roll the dice and try another new one.

"Can you believe this bulls#it? They got my time served all wrong. They keep insisting my start date is July 15, 1983. I was arrested on July 28, 1982. Why can't they get that through their thick skulls?"

"Dude, you're fighting a losing battle. Besides, you got 110 years, what's one more?" Ricky laughed.

Dave ignored him and continued, "They sentence me illegally outside the guidelines, then they can't count my good time accurately, and now they can't even get my start date right."

To any outside observer, whether his sentence ended in 2055 or 2061 didn't make a difference. He'd be long dead by then. But Dave still clung to the dream that he'd get the sentences fixed and be given the chance for parole. Then all these days would matter. And each error he found just brought his obsession with righting it to a boiling point.

Right in the middle of his frothing, he heard the tell-tale monotone beep signaling yet another routine counting activity—head count. Ricky immediately stood up walked out of the cell to the lineup spot. Dave sat there writing on his notepad until the guard finally stuck his head in.

"Uhhh, you planning to escape tonight or something?"

Dave awoke from his trance, "Sorry Bob," he said, throwing his pen on the desk in disgust.

Twice a day like clockwork they counted every inmate, once before breakfast and again before dinner. Days were always the same: Rise for count at 8 a.m., then off to breakfast, usually some powdered eggs and toast, maybe some flavorless oatmeal. After breakfast was shower time. A little grooming and then to the common area for cards, TV or some chit chat. Lunch was at noon and usually involved some form of bologna or Spam. The diet was not exactly what the doctor ordered for a triple bypass survivor. After lunch, they were back in their cells until around 3 p.m. If weather permitted, they'd get an hour outside in the courtyard. Guys would work out, shoot hoops or just mill about. Dave mainly milled. Evening count was at 5 p.m., followed by some meat-and-potatoes type of dinner, usually with a veggie. After dinner, it was back to the cell until lights out at 9 p.m.

Drip, drip, drip, the days droned on in monotony. There were some special occasions, like holidays when they might get a special meal or when a fight broke out or they couldn't count all the heads right. But those weren't really all that special. Even the indoctrination of new inmates, which happened every week and was kind of exciting at first, turned into just another rerun on TV. Some heckling, some cold stares and maybe a little pushing and shoving, but not really too exciting anymore.

"Dave, I need to you verify my count," Bob said. Bob's a seasoned guard. A professional. Tall and broad with a salt-and-pepper mane.

Dave lifted his glasses from his shirt pocket and walked over, grabbing the sheet of paper with the names and numbers. He walked down the aisle and double-checked the count. This was fairly normal practice. The guards would pick their favorites and give them a little extra power (and work). Not only was Dave not a troublemaker, but he was a coalition-builder, a peace-maker. This, along with his wealth of cigarettes and canteen credits, made him popular with most inmates and guards alike.

"I got all thirty-seven, Bob," he confirmed, handing the paper back to him.

"All right, guys," Bob yelled, "single file to the mess!" His voice echoed in the narrow, brightly lit hall. The giant steel door made its usual buzzing sound and began its slow slide as all the inmates turned to their left, almost in unison, and shuffled out. Except Dave, who lingered back.

"So Bob, I'm going to be getting a package from my mom this week." Dave pulled two packs of smokes from the pocket of his loose-fitting jumpsuit and reached out to hand off the bung.

"Got something good coming?" Bob asked, grabbing the smokes. "You sure this is just a two-pack job?"

"Nothing too important. Just some socks and underwear," he revealed with a smirk.

"More Chivas?"

"I'm upping my game a bit. Single malt," Dave replied.

"Okay, Dave. Enjoy your dinner."

Walking into the big, open mess hall, Dave quickly surveyed the room. Everything seemed to be in order. The chow line to the left had twenty or so of the guys slowly moving along, their brown plastic trays pushing along the stainless steel rails. The rectangular tables were arrayed in their usual pattern, and the cliques were all in their usual spots. The skinheads had their four tables closest to the bathrooms. For obvious reasons, the African-Americans were farthest away from them, at the other corner of the room. Next to them were the older white guys, Dave's preferred group even though he wasn't really that old. The Cubans and Latinos swarmed all the tables in the center of the room. They weren't all one gang, but they all got along better with each other than with the other groups. And back near the skinheads were the young white guys, who were always being taunted or recruited depending on whether there was fresh meat to be had.

Speaking of which, newbies always stuck out in the mess hall. They were hesitant, cautious as they looked for an available seat. Pecking order is everything. Sit in the wrong spot and you'd find your tray thrown across the hall and your butt on the floor. Whether they were new to prison or just new to this prison, they seemed to instinctively know to wait and see how things sorted out before settling in.

But today something was different. One of the new guys didn't fit the usual pattern.

"Who's the giant jitterbug jawing with Stoney?" Dave asked his Cuban buddy John Vincente, who had sidled up next to him in the chow line.

The tall, dark-haired John answered with a chuckle, "You mean Tiny? I hear he was sent down from Tallahassee. Almost choked some guard to death up there."

"Wonderful," Dave lamented, unsmiling. He went through the chow line and took his usual spot, keeping tabs on the big-guy's whereabouts.

Tiny never actually sat down during chow; he carried his tray around and moved amongst his clan's tables, talking loudly and forcefully with his brothers. It was clear to Dave this guy was sniffing out the alphas of his group. He'd seen this many times before. Normally, when a guy comes in peacocking like this there's a brutal fight within two days. But normally it wasn't the big guys who stirred up the trouble. Dave's intuition told him three-hundred pounds of alpha was going require a novel approach. And when his peripheral vision noticed Josie, one of the older black guys, pointing Tiny in his direction, he knew he'd have to improvise that approach immediately.

Dave kept his eyes on his food and kept eating, trying to look natural as his mind hurriedly ran through scenarios and approaches. *If he wants lottery tickets, that's cool. If he wants a favor, I'll go along as long as he seems willing to quid pro quo. I'm sure he doesn't want drugs, Josie would have told him I don't do that in here.* Tiny's ten second walk wasn't nearly long enough.

"Hey little man, I hear you got smokes."

Everyone at Dave's table paused their eating and looked up at the bald giant. Dave just kept eating and ignored him.

"Hey," Tiny barked louder, "I said I hear you got smokes."

Dave slowly looked up to engage. His face and neck began to feel warm, so he flipped his mental switch to repress his instincts, which were way more flight than fight.

"I sure do," he replied calmly.

"Gimme some smokes," Tiny insisted as he held out his hand.

Dave noticed his hand was relatively small in proportion to the rest of him, especially his barrel chest and Popeye forearms. He snickered to himself as he imagined maybe that's how he got his nickname. *Better not say that one*, he thought.

"How many and what you got for 'em?" Dave asked as he balled up his napkin and threw it on his plate with a bit of irritation. He figured he already knew the answer, but it was worth asking just in case.

"Whatever you got, and I'll pay you back later." That was code for "and I won't kick your ass later." A couple of the older guys at the end of the table picked up their trays and headed for the exit. Dave paused and took a breath, never breaking eye contact.

"What's your name, friend?"

"Tiny."

"That certainly fits," Dave smirked. "Would you like to have a seat, Tiny?"

"No. Gimme the d@mn smokes!" Now the whole lunchroom became silent.

"I don't know how they do things up in Tallahassee these days, Tiny, but that's not how it works down here." Dave's voice was steady and clear, and he purposely looked at Tiny the way he wanted to look at Tocco all those years earlier—with a twinge of arrogance. "Down here, it's not about who you are, but who you know. I don't know you yet. So have a seat." Dave added some intensity when he said "have a seat."

Tiny's angry face melted and he assumed a slack-jawed look of disbelief. He shook his head and turned away, muttering, "This guy's gonna regret that. D@mn fool shoulda give me my smokes," as he strutted back over to his posse.

The guys at Dave's table went back to eating, no one saying a word. Dave looked over to Josie, who gave Dave a little salute to say "I'm sorry I had to do that." Dave nodded back at him.

"I think I'm going to get a new roommate," Ricky chuckled. No one else laughed.

"What's the plan?" asked his old partner, Ed McCabe.

"I'm gonna give him some smokes," Dave avowed matter-of-factly.

"Yeah, right," Ed replied with a fake laugh. "You do that and you'll have no friends other than Tiny. I say we jump him in the yard. Send a message quickly."

"You guys never think more than one step ahead, do you? I'm going to have one of the guards put a couple of packs under his pillow before bed tonight." All eyes at the table were trained on Dave like they were watching a magician or something. Dave explained, "He needs to know I can get to him anywhere, anytime. It's far more powerful for your enemy to know you could have taken them out and didn't, than to just take them out." Dave took a sip of his coffee. "And if he ain't that bright, at least the smokes will buy me some time to figure out plan B." His table broke out in nervous laughter.

Dave and Ricky ambled back to their cell. As Dave walked in, he glanced at the scraps of paper on his table and quickly looked away. No way he could handle dealing with that again after his run-in with Tiny. He took a seat on his bed with its thin mattress and stared at the picture of Danny and Dougie hanging below his bunk. It was an old picture, a staged shot from a photographer. It was the last photograph taken before his arrest.

What are they doing right now? He imagined that Danny was at Tae Kwon Do practice and Dougie was playing video games or maybe swimming in the pool. He missed that pool, his house, his old life. He reflected on the past year and a half since he'd seen them and wondered when he'd get to see them again.

Prison living is hard on the heart. If it's not the stress of dealing with the wild animals, then it's the ache of being away from loved ones. But the worst is regret. It picks away. As hard as Dave tries to push it down, he can't escape it. Boredom brings it back. And boredom is his existence.

But there is one refrain that gets him through each day. Like all inmates, he clings to it. He believes it with a faith that makes the most ardent priest look atheist.

Someday.

Someday, I will get out of here.

Chapter Eleven

SURROGATES

1989

Isaiah 9:16 - Those who guide this people mislead them, and those who are guided are led astray.

"Yello," Danny answered the phone in his bedroom with cheer. The voice on the other end was immediately recognizable and not in any way cheery.

"I can't do this no more, Danny; I can't take this no more." His Uncle Mark's cadence was slow.

So much for a relaxing Sunday night, Danny lamented.

Mark and Danny started growing close a couple years earlier. It ignited when Mark had an extra ticket to a Kiss and Ted Nugent concert and no one else to go. It was Danny's first rock concert and he was hooked. From there, they routinely hanged out, listening to music, playing drums, grilling and drinking beer. Separated by only twelve years, Mark became more like a brother to Danny. A massively flawed big brother.

"What happened, man?" Danny asked.

"That b!tch is moving in with him. My daughter is gonna live with that mother f^cker, Danny. I…I can't live with that." Mark's tone was more depressed than angry. Danny preferred angry. He sensed this was going down a bad road.

"Dude, seriously? She's been with him for what, six months?"

"I ain't gonna do it," he said through a sniffle. "I ain't gonna live like this. I'm just calling to say goodbye."

Mark had talked about suicide before. His divorce really put him through a grinder. And his emotional maturity was stunted at around fifteen, so it really hit him harder than it should hit the average twenty-nine-year-old. But the previous discussions were more in jest, more theoretical. This one felt way too serious, too possible.

"What the hell you talking about?" Danny challenged, his heart rate stepping up a notch. "You can't do that to Mo. Not to mention me!"

"I'm sorry, man, I know I'm letting you down. You're stronger than me, so is she. You'll be all right."

"Hey, stop talking like that right now and listen. You need to shut up that voice in your head. It ain't right. You blowing your brains out ain't gonna get back at Ann. It ain't gonna make her pay. It's gonna make your daughter pay. It's gonna make me pay. Grandma. My Mom. Charlie. Kim and Kari. Do I need to keep going?"

Mark's breath was heavy through the phone line. Danny heard sobbing on the other end. "I'm looking at the three-fifty-seven right now. I just…I just don't want this no more."

Danny took a softer tone. "Look, you know that I know what you been through, right? Right?"

"Yeah."

"I know it hurts right now. Remember how bad it hurt a few months ago when you ripped the phone out of the wall? Then remember how much fun we had at the Sweaty Teddy show? It's gonna pass, man."

In reality, Danny didn't understand Mark's reaction. A contentious divorce wasn't something he felt should cause the kind of angst and anger he saw in Mark. But it didn't matter to him. What mattered was getting him through this crash.

"It's just a f^cking see saw, and I'm tired of it, Dano. So I may feel better tomorrow? That ain't gonna change that this assh*le is gonna be raising my daughter with that b!tch."

"So what? So you offing yourself is going to change that? Then they raise her anyway, and you got no say."

"I'm not a good dad anyway. She's better off that I'm gone."

Danny and Mark went back and forth for the better part of an hour. The conversation ebbed and flowed as Danny said whatever he could to keep Mark on the line, to keep him talking. As he chipped away at his heart, slowly, Mark came around and starting talking more sensibly.

"So, here's what I'm going to do," Danny asserted. "I'm going to come over and we're gonna get wasted and eat some burritos. Okay?"

"Yeah."

"I'm not going to show up to find your brains all over the wall, am I?"

"No. I ain't gonna do it."

"You take the bullets out of the gun. Lemme hear 'em hit the table." Danny heard Mark fumbling around and then heard the sound of metal pinging on glass. "Now, put that gun in your closet, okay?"

"All right, I'll see you when you get here."

"Okay, man, be about forty-five."

Danny finished dressing and headed out the door. After a long day at the auto parts store, this isn't exactly the night he had planned. But it didn't matter. If Mark needed him, he was there.

The fall air was growing crisp and sky seemed darker than usual—no moon this night. He sped along the well-trodden path, heading to his home away from home. Finally arriving at Mark's south-side neighborhood, he drove carefully down the crowded, narrow one-way streets looking for an opening. Sunday nights were usually easier to find a parking spot, but the crowded street just added to Danny's frustration. Every minute was another opportunity for Mark to change his mind and do the unthinkable. He settled for a spot a block over and sprinted to the house. Leaping up the concrete steps, he tried to keep his mind from thinking the worst. He twisted the knob, pushed open the door, and snapped his head to the left as he heard a familiar pop!

"What the hell you doing?" Danny asked as he looked in the direction of where the pellet gun was aimed.

"I told ya I wouldn't shoot myself. Didn't say anything about my dining room wall." Mark's eyes were droopy and his face was sallow, partially hidden by the start of his annual beard. He slouched back on his spot on the couch, his usual wall of empty Milwaukee Light cans on the table to his left. His brown hair laid back on his head and was unkempt. He cocked the pellet gun and shot another hole Ann's picture, pinned to the wall.

"You're gonna be pissed if you hit your 901's," Danny challenged as he headed to the kitchen to retrieve a couple of beers.

"I ain't that drunk," Mark shouted over Sammy Hagar's "Red," which blared from the Bose speakers, one of Mark's prized possessions.

Danny headed back into the brightly lit room and sat on the larger couch to Mark's right. The Oakland A's-Blue Jays playoff was on the tube. Danny took a long gulp of beer.

"The A's crushing them again, huh?" Danny asked, trying to make some small talk and keep the mood light.

"Yeah," Mark said, pulling the trigger and putting another hole in his ex's photo. "It's like men against boys."

Before long Ann's picture was barely discernable from all the holes and Danny had his own stack of empties sitting on the table in front of him when the banter started to turn more serious.

"I just wish she'd go away," Mark mused, somehow mistaking his ex for the cause of his depression. "Bitc#es. They're all a bunch of bitc#es."

"Yeah, remember that girl Amy I been telling you about?" Mark nodded. "Stupid slut slept with her ex. I dumped her @ss, right before homecoming, too."

"Cheating bitc#es," Mark spewed, angrily nodding his head. "They're only good for one thing."

Danny nodded in unison. He was starting to believe it himself. He was glad to see Mark's ire. It was preferable to his woe. Mark crushed his can after taking a last sip, and flung it across the room, over the drum set, smacking against the same wall with all the pellet holes in it.

"You're really teaching the wall a lesson," Danny said with a laugh.

"Yeah." Mark reached down and removed the knife from his boot. He stood up and threw it the twenty feet across the rooms. It smacked blunt against the wall and fell to the floor.

"Oooh, you're gonna make that wall mad," Danny chuckled.

"You think it's easy? You try," Mark challenged.

Danny walked over, picked up the knife and walked around the drums. Standing about half the distance of Mark, he got the same result.

"Ha ha ha," Mark bellowed, "give me that thing."

They each took turns trying to stick the remnant of Ann's picture, occasionally getting a gouge or a light stick, only to see gravity pull the knife to the ground. Finally Mark just walked up to the wall and stuck it in overhand fashion, right between her eyes. "That's why I don't throw knives. I just stick 'em!"

While damaging the house was definitely a first, at least this was more like normal Mark—long, droning stories (often repeats), raucous laughter and loud, heavy music. As the baseball game ended and a lull washed over them, a new idea excited Mark's mind.

"You know what we're gonna do?" he stated more than he asked. "We're gonna go and collect my two hundred from Johnny Mitchell."

"Who? What?"

"This friend of Georff's at work had squares for the Cubs series. I won two hundred, and he keeps giving me bulls#it reasons why he ain't paid me yet. It's been two weeks. You and me, we're gonna go collect it." Mark stood up and went to his bedroom, emerging with his 357 Magnum.

"You ain't gonna shoot him, are ya?"

"Not if I don't have to." Mark put the bullets from the table back in the gun and flicked his wrist, closing the barrel. His movements were smooth and quick. You'd never know he'd drank almost twenty beers. He tucked it in his pants at the small of his back and picked up his leather zap gloves from under the table, throwing them to Danny. "You wear these and grab the knife from the wall."

Without hesitation, Danny followed orders. He donned a sweatshirt and put the sand-filled gloves in the pockets. He grabbed the knife, sheathed it and clipped it to his pocket. He spread his legs sideways and thrust his hips forward to stretch out his groin like he did before his Tae Kwon Do classes. They hardly said a word to each other, suiting up and psyching up like soldiers heading into battle.

Mark emerged from the kitchen with three beers suspended in one hand and headed out the door. Danny followed behind and climbed into his bright red Ford Bronco. Mark set two of the beers in the cup holders and popped open the third, chugging about half of it while the Bronco warmed up. He reached around to the boom box in the backseat turning it on, "Highway to Hell" ironically blaring from the speakers.

"Hell Yeeeeeaaaaaahhhhhh!" Mark yelled at the top of his lungs, putting the truck in gear and peeling away from the curb.

Danny's body shivered, but the cool night air wasn't the cause. He opened a beer and drank carefully, always looking around for cops. The drive wasn't too far, about fifteen minutes. Danny hoped Mark would change his mind. As much as he'd trained in the past three years and overcome his insecurities and inferiorities, he'd still never been in a real street fight and didn't really want to be. He certainly didn't want to get into a shootout. But Mark was now Danny's bodyguard, a six-foot-four, two-hundred-forty pound ex-Marine who grew up on the street. Drunk or sober, Danny trusted him. And just like with his old friend Rich, he was willing to overcome his fear and his better judgment anytime Mark asked. But he had never asked him to go to battle like this before.

They pulled up and parallel parked on the street outside a dry cleaners, long since closed. It was eerily quiet out. The yellow tinted streetlights made the scene surreal. Danny put on the zap gloves and pounded his hand with his fist, feeling the pain in his palm and the dull pressure in his sand-covered knuckles.

"Let's do this sh*t!" Danny shouted.

"That's it on the corner," Mark pointed to the three-story tenement. "He's on the second floor. I don't see a light on. We'll go in and go upstairs. I'll knock on the door. If he doesn't have my money or if he tries anything, we kick his @ss. I'll pistol whip him. Only step in if you have to, okay?"

"Got it. Let's rip this son of a bitc#," Danny snarled with intense eyes.

They got out of the truck and walked briskly to the building. The lower door was unlocked and before them was a tall, narrow stairway. Mark went up first, Danny on his heels. At the top landing, Mark stopped and pointed at the door. The lighting was good, so he'd see it was Mark if he looked through his peephole. Danny took a deep breath, feeling his heartbeat in his neck. Mark drew the gun from his back and knocked forcefully on the door. Danny's breathing went shallow and it got so quiet, he could hear the hum of the transformer from the light overhead. They listened intently for signs of life, and Danny's eyes bounced from Mark's to the door and back. Danny shrugged his shoulders. Mark knocked again, harder. Nothing. No answer.

"What we gonna do now?" Danny said quietly. Mark pounded again. Danny's blood pressure began to drop as he realized their battle would not commence that night. Mark stuck the Magnum in his pants and motioned for Danny to depart.

Johnny wasn't home, or at least he was smart enough to not answer the door. Danny was one part relieved and one part disappointed. To be stuck on the edge of something monumental like this was kind of like going up in the airplane, donning the parachute, but not jumping—thrilling, but anticlimactic. Still, Danny felt a sense of power eclipsing anything he'd felt before. Not when he won a martial-arts tournament, not when he got his black belt, not the time at school when all his peers cheered on his kicking demonstration had he felt such a surge of testosterone.

Danny was very fortunate. He had many surrogates who filled in for Dave's absence over the years: Uncle Wayne took him camping and taught him about making fires and working with his hands. Uncle Mike took him fishing. Aunt Sandy had him for sleepovers. She took him to visit Northern Illinois University and encouraged him to go to school. Aunt Debbie was a best friend who made him laugh and tried to keep him from being too macho—the ying to Mark's yang. Aunt Nonie taught him to drive and encouraged his inner thespian. Uncle Charley drove him to and from Four Seasons for years, teaching him how to work and coaching him through rough waters. But in their mutual immaturity, Uncle Mark had the biggest impact, some for better, some for worse.

Believe it or not, the drama of potential suicide and the prospect of life-threatening danger were for the better. He survived them, and they gave Danny experiences most young men from suburbia never get. They brought him a confidence and tenacity that would propel his social life and career once properly focused. But for the worse, Mark's views about women helped embed a flaw in Danny's character. A fault that would later affect his relationships and eventually his eternity.

Chapter Twelve

REGRET

1994

Romans 1:28 – Furthermore, just as they did not think it worthwhile to retain the knowledge of God, so God gave them over to a depraved mind, so that they do what ought not to be done.

Danny pulled up the driveway of Julie's father's house where he and Julie had been staying, and he put the car in park. The sky was gray and gloomy. He knew deep down what he had to do, he was caught. But his mind kept searching for other options, ways to deliver the message that might not be so painful, so potentially permanent.

Danny and Julie met during their sophomore year at college in DeKalb, Illinois, a small oasis in a sea of corn fields. They were placed on the same dorm floor, Grant North, C-Tower. Their first encounter was when Julie popped into his dorm room during move-in week and asked to borrow a pair of scissors. After she left, Danny and his best-friend roommate, Scott Truss, shot each other a look of approval.

Danny quickly discovered they shared an 8 a.m. sociology class that semester. The long walks to and from class afforded them a chance to chat and get to know each other a bit. Danny was attracted to Julie, but the fact that his girlfriend of almost two years also resided on the 5th floor precluded his ability to pursue anything. And he would have likely pursued if given the right opportunity.

Danny's road to becoming a cheat was a long one. In reality, he didn't even consider himself a cheat, like it was such a bad thing. For him, it was the natural behavior of people. When his girlfriend Diane left him to go back to her ex, that was the surprise opening salvo. When Amy cheated on him before homecoming, that became the one-two punch. From his training in the martial arts, he learned sometimes the best defense is a good offense. So his mistrust turned into a "get them before they get me" approach to relationships.

It didn't help that his brain had been hardwired to view women as objects since he was very young. It started very innocently, as most sin does. His dad used to keep a stack of magazines next to the toilet in the upstairs bathroom. One day during a lengthier stay, he reached down to thumb through one of them. When he saw the centerfold, he suddenly started spending a lot more time on the toilet.

He also began to spend a lot more time seeking the attention and affections of girls. In first grade, he got reprimanded several times for chasing his classmates around the playground during recess, trying to plant kisses as they ran away. The thrill of the chase enthralled him.

Unfortunately for Danny, he was young for his grade, smaller than other boys, less cool. This made all his chasing fruitless. And rejection hurts.

One early rejection in particular had a significant impact on Danny. Her name was Honor, and she was as cute as her nickname, Punky. One day in the third grade, he sat around his kitchen table with his mommy, his Aunt Nonie and Aunt Debbie, looking through school pictures. Danny mentioned how much he liked Punky, and the women immediately took interest. "What's she like? Have you asked her to come over? Maybe we could take you to the roller rink?"

As they sat there polishing jewelry, dreaming up potential dates, Danny hatched plan of his own. "Maybe I could give her this ring?" he sheepishly asked, holding up an elegant-looking cocktail ring. The ladies all looked at each other, seeking guidance as to whether or not that was too much for a third grade crush. Eventually, much to Danny's chagrin, they settled on letting him have a gaudy amethyst ring and a promise they'd take him to a movie or out for lunch.

The next day Danny told his plan to Johnny Koo, a recent arrival to the school who Danny befriended. Johnny agreed to help Danny and walk to the classroom across the hall to present the gift to Punky. The butterflies were crawling out of his stomach as he gave Johnny the signal to go, carefully watching the teacher to make sure she didn't catch them. Johnny was gone so long, or so it seemed, that Danny was sure he had gotten in trouble. Finally, he heard some giggling, then Johnny came running back with a big embarrassed grin, his cheeks swelling on both sides of his face.

"What'd she say?" Danny asked in a whisper.

"They just laughed," he replied. "I had to get out of there because Mrs. Falls saw me."

No sooner had Johnny gotten the words from his mouth, then in walked Mrs. Falls. "I believe this belongs to you," she said, handing the ring back to Johnny. Laughter erupted in the room as Johnny shook his head and pointed over to Danny. Danny looked down at the desktop and just wished he would wake up.

Embarrassment does one of two things to you. It either makes you shy and sheepish or it brings out a determination. That moment solidified Danny's already considerable reputation as a dork, and it also etched in him a resolve that would thrive for the next fifteen years. He would not forever be the awkward, embarrassed nerd. He would figure out how to approach, attract, and seduce.

Unfortunately, his experiences with objectifying women didn't end with those early Playboy magazines. They were reinforced with magazines and movies at virtually all of his uncle's houses. And when his mom got remarried, his soon-to-be stepdad bequeathed his stack of raunchy magazines to Danny, saying, "I guess I won't be needing these anymore." With access like that, who needs Al Gore to invent the internet? His mind was awash in smut.

And since he didn't have the courage to risk suffering another humiliation at school, he tested his powers of seduction in other venues instead. His cousins Kimmy and Kari had a friend, Alicia. Unfettered by his hometown reputation, he found some success with her. He was able to flirt and get some positive feedback. He was able to get her phone number and even eventually get her to agree to "go out" with him, although they never actually had a date outside of his Uncle Wayne's house. It's tough to date when you're thirteen and your "girlfriend" lives an hour away.

But other opportunities presented themselves. His next girlfriend came along when he was down with his grandmother visiting his dad in Florida. Swimming in the ocean after the visit one afternoon, along swam Debbie, an older girl from Fort Wayne, Indiana. She and Danny spent a couple of hours bobbing up and down in the ocean, talking. They agreed to meet up by the pool after dinner where they made out in the hot tub and awkwardly fondled each other until midnight. After that trip, they maintained a long-distance relationship through letters and phone calls. Eventually, Danny even convinced his aunt to drive him for a weekend visit in Fort Wayne. There, he found that having was not as fun as chasing, so they split up after the visit.

There were others, but he eventually moved on to Diane and then Amy, where he learned that losing is worse than having. So when he started dating Allison at seventeen, she unwittingly walked into the dichotomy he had become. On one side, he was fun and affable. On the other, he was sneaky and selfish. He learned to get along with everyone, young or old, cool or nerd, black or white. He could seemingly adapt to any situation. But it was a mirage. He was really unfeeling and distrusting, always looking to see if there was something better, someone else to chase. Someone else so that he wouldn't lose.

Fittingly, Danny and Allison broke up that fall sophomore semester. Danny experienced strike three as Allison started taking interest in another guy on the dorm floor, affirming his distrust, not realizing he was mostly responsible for it. So when Julie cornered him at a party one evening after the break-up and laid a big kiss on him, she inherited that legacy.

But sitting in his car in her dad's driveway, two and a half years later, this was his first inkling he didn't want that anymore. He was tired of the chase. He just wanted her. If only he had realized it a couple of months earlier.

How do you tell someone you love that you've betrayed them, but you'd still like to work things out? One way or the other, life was about to change. People who he grew to know and love beyond Julie, like her parents and brother and best friend Dave, would all find out. Where would he live? Would they ever talk to him again?

Danny felt the weight of being alone, the uncertainty of his future. All of this for the momentary thrill of the chase. An old enemy he couldn't escape covered him like a blanket once again. He took a deep breath, stepped out of the car and took the long walk of shame into the house, down to the basement, to count the cost for his failings.

Chapter Thirteen

ENOUGH IS ENOUGH

1999

Colossians 3:21 – Fathers, do not embitter your children, or they will become discouraged.

Dave spent enough time between Las Vegas and Acapulco to know the one rule of gambling. The house always wins. As he thumbed through the stack of lottery tickets checking for winners, he knew one thing for sure. He'd already won.

"No winners here, boys," he said to a chorus of groans. "Get your numbers to Ed if you're in for the next round." As the crowd gathered in the common area broke up, Dave looked over to Nick Colozzo, "Except for you, of course," he winked.

As his mother's money dried up after the auto businesses closed, Dave needed to find other sources of income. Working in the mailroom or the laundry room only netted three dollars per hour, and Dave had never worked for an hourly wage his whole life. He was always the boss. So he concocted a scheme.

The game started out quite simple. Dave and Ed bought and sold tickets to the Florida State Lottery: Pick 3, Pick 4 and Lotto. They had connections on the outside buy the tickets and sneak them in through various means. Originally, they tried to convince their cellmates to keep the tickets on the outside and avoid all the hassle of smuggling them in. But that didn't fly; they had to see the tickets to trust they were real. For their trouble, Dave and Ed kept a 10% cut (only 5% for their buddies). In the rare event of a winner, they got the tickets back out to their proxies who would cash them in and deposit the money to Dave's prison account. He could then transfer the money to winner's account. It all worked quite well with only a few hiccups requiring bribes along the way.

But when Colozzo came to the prison a few years prior, Dave concocted a more complex game. A game that, so to speak, got Dave back in the game.

Nick Colozzo was the head of the Gambino crime syndicate. When he arrived to the prison, he immediately had a following with the inmates and tremendous sway with the guards. In order to ingratiate himself with Colozzo, Dave proposed that Nick play along with their lottery. But there was a wrinkle. The lottery ticket numbers Colozzo played were actually messages, sent in code. Dave convinced Colozzo that he could encrypt messages which could be sent through unwitting intermediaries to Colozzo's underlings. This would keep him in charge of his syndicate and be virtually untraceable if ever intercepted. All Dave wanted in return was Colozzo's friendship. A peace between potential rivals. After some initial skepticism, he eventually agreed to partner with Dave.

Danny was one of the go-betweens. For years, he played along with the game, receiving and holding tickets, then mailing them to wherever Dave asked, whenever he asked. He didn't ask a lot of questions about what was going on, figuring it was some scheme to make a buck. He didn't really want to know. Their relationship had drifted into the superficial. The mundane. This lottery ticket game was his one last vestige of trying to please his daddy. A way to mollify his guilt over his growing disdain.

It's not like Dave did anything specific to elicit this feeling in Danny. Life just got busier and more complicated, and time more precious. As that happened, he began to dread hearing the monotone recording of the bi-weekly phone calls: "You have received a call from…Dave…an inmate at the Dade County Correctional Institute. To accept charges, press one." Each ten minute, ten dollar phone call was predictably the same: pleasantries; catch up on what's been going on; talk about the Cubs or Bears; the one-minute warning; then the I-love-yous and goodbye—preferably before they were suddenly cut off.

Being annoyed by the timing and inconvenience of a collect call or by the hassle of mailing lottery tickets is one thing. But an unexpected favor one day wound up being the straw that broke the camel's back. And it put their relationship on a whole different footing.

"Will you get me the jar of sweet potatoes?" Julie asked.

"I don't see them."

"They're up there, keep looking."

Danny fumbled around in the cabinet, moving jars and cans. "I think we're out."

Julie walked over and reached into the cabinet almost without looking, emerging with the jar she requested. "I swear, you couldn't find a hat if it was on your head."

Danny laughed and shook his head. He grabbed a bib and put it around Zachary's neck, trying to be helpful in some small way.

Danny and Julie's relationship survived his betrayal. Danny went into the basement that day and ashamedly admitted his failure. Julie had a normal, healthy, angry reaction. She kicked him out of her dad's house and he went to live with a friend. But he didn't give up. Letters were written. Yells were directed over phone lines. Tears. Apologies. And love. Julie sensed a sincerity in Danny, a real willingness to repent. The forgiveness wasn't easy for her to extend, but trust was rebuilt day by day, date by date. Danny vowed to himself that his days of running around were over. He loved her too much, and he was grateful for her heart of forgiveness.

Within two years they were married, way too soon according to Danny's mom. He reminded her that she got married at eighteen; he was twenty-three. "Look how my marriage turned out," she reminded him. But Danny wasn't worried. His aspirations were pretty simple: be with someone he loved, raise a family and do something significant in his life. Be someone others admire and look up to. Pretty standard stuff.

After the marriage came the house. After the house came Zachary. And with it all came the challenge of just keeping up. They found themselves often tired and sleepless, with a piece of their heart lying in a crib, crying in the middle of the night. They both just wanted to soothe it and hoped they wouldn't screw it up too bad. It was in the midst of this newfound chaos and emotional rollercoaster when the call came in.

Danny walked over and answered the phone. He rolled his eyes when he heard the robotic voice, "Hello, you have received a call from…" He really didn't want to talk right now. The Bears game was on and he was trying to do whatever he could to lighten Julie's considerable load—or at least to look like he was trying. But when he heard the name and the voice, he suddenly became very curious "…Ed McCabe…an inmate at the Dade County Correctional Institute. To accept charges, press one."

"That's weird," Danny said. Julie turned away from Zach, the sweet potatoes oozing from the corners of his mouth, to see the puzzled look on Danny's face.

Danny had only met Ed McCabe a handful of times he could remember. There were vague memories of him being around at the pool parties before the arrest, and he met him a couple of times while visiting his dad in Florida. Ed was a friendly guy with Danny. He was very complimentary of Dave, always talking up how great a guy he was, how he got railroaded. Danny didn't know much about Ed's involvement in the whole drug and kidnapping situation. But he knew enough to know he wasn't a choir boy. He was lean and strong looking, a bit rough around the edges. And getting a call out of the blue from him was unprecedented. He wondered if maybe his dad had had a heart attack or something.

"Hello," he said, almost as if asking a question.

"Danny," he greeted, "Hey, man, it's Ed McCabe."

"Hey, Ed. What's going on?" Danny's voice was slow and somewhat skeptical sounding.

"Thanks for taking the call, man. Your dad gave me your number. I got good news this week. I'm going to be getting out next month." Ed sounded as excited as you might expect he'd be.

"Wow, you're getting out. That's great, man, but why are you telling me about it?" The look on Julie's face began to mirror Dan's, furrowed brow and frown.

"Well, your dad thought maybe you could help me out when I get sprung. After seventeen years, I don't have a lot of friends and family left."

Danny's mind raced with emotions. Part of him felt pity for Ed. Part of him felt jealous. Why couldn't his dad be getting out? But the biggest part of him reflected what he knew was going to be going through Julie's head once she heard the whole story—fear. He stared into Zachary's innocent blue eyes as he sat in his high chair, playing with his sippy cup. The risk was not worth any reward he could conjure.

"You know, Ed, I'm happy for you getting out, but I don't even really know you. I'm sorry, man, but I'd really appreciate it if you didn't call here again."

There was an awkward pause, "Okay, man. Sorry to bother you."

"Thanks, Ed. Take care."

"What the hell was that?" Julie asked before he even put the handset back on the wall.

As he explained it to her, they began to feed off each other's emotions, and they got madder and madder. *How dare he give out our information to his cronies? What if he has our address? He could just show up one day.* It wasn't a week later when he got to vent their frustrations. His hands began to sweat as he heard the robotic introduction.

"Dad," Danny pronounced in a stern voice as he heard the telltale click connecting their call.

"Hey buddy…"

"Hey, look, we gotta problem here. Why the hell did you give our number to Ed McCabe?"

"Well, I knew he could use a friend on the outside…"

"Look, Dad," Danny interrupted in his stern voice, "I have a family now that I have to worry about. You make sure Ed knows he is NEVER to call here again. And you are NEVER to give out our number or our address or anything to any of your friends. Understand?"

"Okay. I'm sorry, I didn't realize…"

"And another thing. I'm done with the lottery tickets. Don't send me any more. I'm too busy and have too much going on to be a part of whatever it is you're doing."

"Okay," Dave said stoically after a short pause. He wasn't used to being talked to this way and certainly never from Danny. He felt a pit in his chest worse than any heartburn he suffered. In a sheepish voice he continued, "Look, son, I'm sorry. I should have talked to you before doing anything like that. It won't happen again."

Now Danny, the perennial peacemaker, began to feel bad, too. "Thank you. Sorry to be so harsh, but I just need to be clear about it."

"Oh, it's clear."

After the call, Dave went back to his cell and laid on his bed for the rest of the night. He wasn't as bothered by losing one of his lottery messengers as he was that he'd overstepped his bounds. If only he was able to see him, he could work things out. He looked up at the picture of him and Danny from the last visit, over four years ago. *I wonder if I'll ever see him again?* He was so calloused from the years in prison that he didn't shed a tear about it. But he did add another regret to his long list. Another regret that, for every passing day without a visit, he'd believe was his fault. Another regret he'd have to learn to push down and ignore.

Chapter Fourteen

THE WAY OF THE FOOL

2002

Proverbs 14:12 – There is a way that appears to be right, but in the end it leads to destruction.

The streetlight shone through the side windows framing the front door, but that's not what was keeping Danny awake as he laid on the living room couch. It was the idea that kept rolling around in his soul. It was at the same time both terrifying and exhilarating. A scheme he had never seriously considered before.

A few hours earlier, he and Julie had another fight. In their over six years of marriage and eleven years together, fights were normal. But in recent months, they'd escalated in frequency and intensity. Regardless of the specifics, the root of each fight was the same—unmet expectations.

Danny's expectations were that he would provide for the family and pursue his career and personal aspirations while Julie tended to the household. To him, it was the whole point of having a stay-at-home mom. They would go on vacations and do normal family things, but his highest aim, his ultimate goal was to climb the ladder and run a large business. This would bring wealth and comfort, and most of all admiration and respect. He got his first taste for this several years prior when his boss told him he'd put his name in as someone who could ascend to CEO one day. This astounded Danny; the idea had never crossed his mind before. But the appetite was whet and his hunger stoked. Following that, Danny took jobs which stretched him and pulled at his time, even at his thoughts. He craved respect, and the more he found it at work, the less he was able to find it at home.

For Julie's part, she wanted a partner, not just a breadwinner. She wanted a man who wanted to be around her and spend time with the family as much as he wanted to bring home the bacon. She wanted to feel important, loved. Love is not the vibe given by a man whose mind is focused on himself.

This could work, he tried to convince himself. *I could give up the house, half the 401k, half of my future income and I'd still be pretty wealthy. I could move anywhere I want. I could move to corporate headquarters in Connecticut like they've been wanting. I could even go to China.*

China. China was taking him down. It lured him with its mysterious culture and stroked him with attention and respect. She stroked him with her attention and respect.

Danny first met Kari Lee when on a trip to Xiamen to visit his company's repair center there. The task was to work with local government officials to get the approvals for opening a joint venture business with another aerospace company. Danny had to meet with the local governor and discuss the plan and process. Kari was the translator.

Kari was an average-looking Chinese woman, not particularly attractive or mysterious. She had short black hair, an average build and some mild remnants of acne on her cheeks. She dressed very conservatively and had little in the way of a figure from what Danny could tell. She greeted Danny outside the governor's office and introduced herself. Through the meeting, he did his job and she did hers, always smiling. She seemed to glow with an energy; her eyes were bright with life.

Later that night, as they gathered around the large round table for dinner, she sat to Danny's left and helped him understand the customs and culture. Danny was grateful she was there, not only for the translations and lessons, but also as the only one there who was interesting and genuinely interested in him. She seemed so curious: *How did someone so young get to be in such a position to be meeting with the governor?* She unintentionally stroked his ego with each probing question, making him feel like a king.

When the dinner ended, everyone said their goodbyes and departed. Danny figured he'd never see any of them again. But Satan has a way of picking at scabs. A couple of months later when he was back in Xiamen for an industry conference, guess who he happened to bump into?

"Hello, Mr. Doomberg," Kari said, mispronouncing his name.

Danny ignored it, finding it cute. "Kari!" he smiled. "I didn't know you'd be at this conference." Even though Danny was there with his counterpart from the joint venture company, he was elated to see a familiar face.

"Yes," she said, smiling and bowing her head, "my job is to meet with the companies and help them to make sure they understand why to do business in Xiamen."

"That's great," Danny admitted as they walked along the tall echoing hallway outside the convention center. "Will you be going to the dinner tonight?"

"Yes. It is okay I join you tonight?"

"Absolutely! I could use the company and the translation."

"Very good," she said with her usual glow, "now I will have a good night instead of a boring one."

Despite being at a table for ten, their dinner was intimate, personal, private. Danny and Kari talked about their lives. Kari was married, but it was an arranged marriage. She felt disconnected from her husband, who was lazy and liked to play video games. Danny shared that he had two little boys and a baby girl on the way. But he too felt distance growing in his marriage. They talked about their favorite foods, career aspirations and dream vacations, only occasionally pausing to listen to a short speech by a dignitary.

After dinner, Danny and his associate were to meet up with some employees of the joint venture company to see the town. Kari was invited along. They went out to clubs, drinking and dancing. Danny was quite a seasoned drinker, but he was amazed at how much some of the locals could drink. They went from bar to bar, drinking beer, doing shots, and carrying on like teenagers.

Toward the end of the night, he sat at the bar feeling tired and too old. He looked out to the dance floor where Kari and her girlfriends were still dancing. Something about their spirit caused Danny's mind to go where he knew it shouldn't. But he didn't stop it. He imagined himself out there with her, slowly dancing, holding each other closely. He imagined what it would be like to kiss her. To be with her. To live with her.

An hour later, when the taxi pulled up to his hotel, he asked, "Will I see you again before I leave?"

"I will come by the company tomorrow."

Danny headed up to his room and felt the strange mixture of excitement and regret. On one hand, the thrill of the chase, like an old dealer to a junkie, called to him. On the other, Julie and the kids. He passed out, fantasies and fears abounding.

A mere five hours later, still drunk, he headed out to work. All of his friends from the night before were there, looking somehow no worse for the wear. Through the day, he went through the motions, having his meetings, planning the new operation, and drinking lots of water. But his mind was quick to wander. Any time the front door opened, he hoped she was there. He was captivated. He felt like the most important person in the world when she was around, like the president of a large company.

She stopped by later that day, and they got to talk for a while. They exchanged emails and vowed to write each other. Danny and his business partner left the city and headed home. But Danny couldn't help but feel melancholy about leaving. It felt like he was leaving home, never to return. Instead, he was headed to a place with stress and strife. A place where he wasn't so special.

In the weeks and months after that visit, Danny's heart grew further from home and closer to the fantasy of Kari. They exchanged emails regularly. The bitter taste of home contrasted with the sweet words he'd get in his inbox. Julie could feel the betrayal, but she couldn't quite put her finger on it. He was different, distant, rude, inconsiderate, selfish. Finally this fateful night, it blew up.

Danny returned home after spending the day at their friend Dave's, watching football, drinking beer. Julie laid in bed reading and exhausted. He could tell by her countenance she was mad. He tried to meekly change clothes and ignore the elephant in the room. But that's not Julie's style.

"Nice of you to stay out all day. I got Lucas to the immediate care. He's got an ear infection, in case you care."

"Oh man, again? That sucks."

"You know what sucks? Doing all this by myself, while pregnant! It would be nice if you cared for us as much as your precious football."

Danny felt anger overcome his weakened inhibitions. "You know, I spent all day yesterday building that damn swing set. Is it really so bad that I get a Sunday to decompress?"

"When do I get a day to decompress? Why to do you get one but I don't?"

Back and forth they escalated, both too angry and immersed to budge. Julie felt unloved and drained. Danny felt disrespected and laden with unfair expectations. The pent-up pressure exploded.

"You are being completely unreasonable!" he continued. The boys slept in the room next door, and he knew he shouldn't be loud. But he couldn't help himself.

"Quiet down," Julie sternly replied. "How on earth can you think it's okay to spend every god d@mn Sunday at Dave's watching football and getting drunk while I take care of the kids and this baby in here? I don't know if you're a sociopath or just stupid!"

"You know, I'm sick of this 'I do everything and you do nothing' attitude of yours! You think you're so much better than me. Like you're such a good person and I'm a piece of s#it. I provide everything for this family, and I do chores around here, too. Just because you like to stay home and go to bed early doesn't make you a better person."

"That's a good one! What do you do around here, Danny, what? List it off for me, please. You think taking out the garbage and doing the dishes on occasion gets you some kind of great husband award? You're a joke."

"I can't take this s#it anymore; you don't fight fair. You don't listen, and you don't really want to compromise. You can have the effing bed. See you later." He stormed out of the room with red face and clenched jaw.

As Danny was propping pillows and getting a blanket for the couch, his adrenaline rush resurged as he heard the footsteps coming down the stairs.

"You've got coconut balls to tell me I don't want to compromise. I'm carrying our baby. I haven't been able to have a beer for seven months. I don't see you compromising that, do I?" Danny just sat on the couch and stared blankly at the wall. Julie continued, "You travel all the time, get to eat out, see the world. Guess who's back here taking care of your kids? Guess who's going to doctor appointments and grocery shopping and story time at the library? So when you're here on a weekend, I'm glad to just have you around most of the time. I'm not asking you to remodel the house. I just need a break. You have no idea how stressful it is to deal with a two- and four-year-old all friking day. So don't try to tell me I'm being unreasonable. That's some bulls#it you made up so you can feel better about ditching us. Again!" And she turned and went back up to her bedroom.

Danny stared at the blinds covering the big square living room window, his heart beating hard and chest moving with each deep breath. He wanted to go up and grab a suitcase and just pack it and go, rent a hotel room, maybe go to Dave's. Instead he sat there in a fog, rerunning the argument in his mind. He was sure he was right. Each rerun just reaffirmed it as he blended the memories to his advantage.

I just can't take this anymore, he concluded. *I deserve better than this. I deserve peace. I deserve to have some free time. I deserve respect.*

He reached over and turned off the lamp and laid down on the couch. This was the first time he'd ever slept on the couch after a fight. And he vowed it would be his last.

I deserve respect, kept replaying in his mind. And China called to him. *I could get a divorce. It would be painful to be away from the kids, but it could work. One weekend with me, another with her. I've got to find a way to get out of this mess. I've got to find a way to get back to China.*

Chapter Fifteen

EPIPHANY

2003

Romans 6:23 – For the wages of sin is death, but the gift of God is eternal life in Christ Jesus our Lord.

As is typical for a family with three little ones, it could be hard to get out the door on time, especially on the weekend mornings. That they were up, showered, dressed and on the road on a Sunday morning in September was weird enough in itself. The fact they were headed to church and looking forward to it is what was really amazing. But an even bigger surprise awaited them on the drive.

Danny never made it back to China. Shortly after their horrible fight, his job in China abruptly ended. The business partner pulled out unexpectedly. His opportunities to see Kari were stymied, and part of Danny was grateful for that. Over time, their emails trailed off to nothing.

Baby Sophia soon arrived and brought joy and new challenges as Julie struggled with postpartum depression. Normally that kind of stress on a tenuous relationship would drive a wedge and deepen a divide, but something in Danny responded well to the challenge. On the brink of sinking fully into the cesspool of his own ego and selfish desire, God began to get Danny's attention. Well, He'd really been setting it up for years.

Shortly after their marriage in 1996, Danny and Julie moved into nice two-story house on Waterview Road. The subdivision was being developed by Julie's then-best friend's husband, and they scored a great deal on the spec home. The houses were packed together like sardines, so getting to know their neighbors was inevitable. Not that Danny or Julie were hermits or anything, but they didn't generally feel the need to widen their social circle. Regardless, they did. Jeremy and Tamara lived in the tri-level house on the cul-de-sac to their north. It started as these things typically do, with waves to each other while mowing the lawn or departing for work. The ladies would chat about recipes and whatnot. If Danny needed a tool, he would stop over and see if Jeremy had it. But it really sparked into a friendship the summer of 1998 when Danny mentioned to Jeremy that they were expecting their first baby. Turned out so were they.

From there it blossomed, bonding through the birth of their first and second kids. Spending hours upon hours at the play gym, the library or just hanging out on the weekends. They got to know each other's extended families and friends. They went on vacations. They shared each others' trials and worked through them together.

It was in midst of this seemingly normal friendship when something started to stir in Danny. Jer and Tam were religious but not obnoxiously so. They liked to talk about God or about their church, but it came up casually, without alarm or superiority. Danny enjoyed talking about God. Well, more like debating about Him. He had developed some militantly agnostic beliefs through the course of his life. He believed God existed, but he had no doubt that all the world's religions were just grasping at straws in trying to fathom the unfathomable. People who believed in a religion were just needing a salve to soothe their fears or a club in which to belong. The opioid for the masses.

His beliefs were, just like everyone's, born out of his experiences. His mom grew up Catholic, and his dad grew up as a non-practicing Lutheran. Both of them believed they didn't need religion in their lives. There was a leather-bound Bible on the bookshelf, but the only time it ever came out was when Danny's curiosity got the better of him. It was quickly shelved once the awkward King James English sufficiently bored or confused him.

The proliferation of the televangelists during his youth didn't help him either. Out of morbid curiosity, Danny would occasionally watch them peddle their snake oil. The words of his mother would rise up over their ostentatious emotional appeals: "The Bible was created by men in power to control other people and take their money." These so-called religious men seemed to give ample credence to her assertion.

Sleepovers at his grandma and grandpa's afforded him the only opportunities to actually set foot in a church. He probably only went ten times over the course of his life, being roused before he wanted to and carted to the stodgy, slow-paced services full of ritual and creeds. This obviously did nothing to stir in Danny a desire to be a Christian or a Catholic. And what's the difference anyway? All those religions, those denominations, were just doing the same thing. Trying to put their spin on the creator so they could be the ones with the power. They could be the ones in control. No one was going to control Danny. He would be in charge of his own mind, his own fate.

But still, Jer and Tam had some interesting ideas about God, forgiveness, mercy, and grace. They'd talk about Christianity vs agnosticism, about God's nature and His will for His creation. It tended to be good-natured and light-hearted. And it was effective. Their approach allowed Danny to be open-minded and hear their arguments. And it made him uncomfortable. They really challenged his view of the world. So much so, he stayed up late one night writing down his beliefs about the nature of the universe and God:

> "God exists. I believe this based on the immensity and complexity of the universe and how it's so perfectly designed to work. God created and set the world in motion and is watching from afar to see what we will create of it. Will we ultimately evolve and create something he would approve of or will we descend into evil like terrorists? God does not intervene in the world. I suppose he might if we ever got so close to destroying it that it could never recover if he didn't. But he doesn't. And he doesn't care about whether I believe in him or not. He cares about whether I'm trying to be a good person. And if he won't accept me as I am, then I don't want any part of him anyway."

Jer and Tam were trying to crack a hard nut. His shell had been calloused with twenty years of heartache, with the indoctrination of science and engineering, and with the biased and sensationalist news stories depicting the worst of religion. Even Danny's own duplicity reinforced that shell.

When their firstborn, Zachary, was coming due, Danny and Julie tried to get religious. They went back to Gloria Dei Lutheran, the church where they were married, and they became members. They went to services for a couple of years, even on 9/11 when they were needing answers to the evil that befell that day. But for Danny, it never took. He went through the motions, but his heart was not in it. Occasionally he'd hear something useful in a sermon. But for the most part, being there just highlighted his hypocrisy. He was doing this for show, for Julie, or something. He didn't believe this stuff. His being there was no better than the people who espoused real belief and went on being bad people anyway.

So in 2003 when Julie started going to Northeast Christian Church and reporting back her enthusiasm, Danny was highly resistant. "It's so different than Gloria Dei," she encouraged. "The music is modern, and the sermons have humor and connect with real life. It's a little weird with people raising their hands when singing and stuff, but I'd really like you to check it out."

For weeks, months, he denied her. "Sunday is my day to relax," he pressed. Truth was, he had little interest in going through the motions. He knew what he believed and there was no point in pursuing it further. But eventually, for some reason, he relented.

As reported, Northeast Christian was different. It certainly wasn't like the Catholic services his grandparents took him to during his sleepovers or the similar-feeling Lutheran ones either. No Apostles' Creed. No stilted reading of the word. The music was good, if not a bit cheesy. But the sermons, that's what impressed Danny the most. These weren't some dry, esoteric ramblings about events that happened thousands of years ago. These were practical, relevant teachings tying those biblical events to real life. Practical teachings about right and wrong, about how to be a better father, husband, leader, man.

Danny encountered truths there he knew in his gut were real and good. Jesus taught to love your enemy. *Yes! This is the only real solution to all the strife in the Middle East. The only way to diffuse grudges so deep, they're almost a part of our DNA.* He learned that pride is what leads to a person's downfall and that God will exalt the humble. He realized the truth that you can tell what a person loves by where they put their money. Or that looking lustfully at a woman is just as bad as physically cheating. He knew that one first hand. These were radical new ways of looking at life and at God, but only radical and new for him.

Those truths were hidden in that King James Bible on his bookshelf as a kid, in plain sight if only he would have really looked.

One particular truth wormed its way into Danny's soul a few months after starting at Northeast. It was in a sermon delivered by Pastor Hume and it was blunt—something which would have closed Danny's heart and mind normally. But thanks to Jer and Tam and a myriad of other situations in his life, this time he was open. This time, he was really hearing it for the first time. He was seeing its truth in himself.

> "Evil people and good people apart from Christ will both be in the same place after they die. Let me say it again, evil people and good people apart from Christ will both be in the same place after they die. We like to think we're good people. Well, better than most, right? But even the best person, apart from Christ, is imperfect. And God, who is perfect, can't abide with the imperfect. So when we sin, we can't be with God. Romans 6:23 tells us the wages of sin is death, but the gift of God is eternal life in Christ Jesus. Wages are something you earn. You earn death by disobeying God and rejecting his son. But the gift of God—something you can't earn—is eternal life through His Son."

Danny was mesmerized by the teaching. In the past, what Danny heard in sermons like this was something like, "Obey God and believe in Jesus or you're going to hell." It was a shallow fear-based threat to coerce people to conform to Christianity. This time he heard something completely different. He heard "you are not perfect," and he agreed. He heard "God is perfect," and he agreed. It also made complete sense to him that something perfect would itself become imperfect if it united with imperfection. Good cannot abide with evil. He also heard, and for the first time believed, that heaven must be a gift. It's not something you can strive for and earn by being good enough. It must be something that is given. And like a gift, it must be accepted, opened.

Shortly after hearing that and letting it have its way with his calloused shell, the church started a series based on Rick Warren's book *A Purpose Driven Life*. Each week, they were to read one short chapter a day, and then they would hear a sermon on those chapters each Sunday. On September 21st, 2003, after they'd gotten their three little ones ready and out the door, Danny read Chapter 7 as Julie drove the family to Northeast. In it, Rick Warren challenged him to give his life over to Christ. It read:

> "Right now, God is inviting you to live for his glory by fulfilling the purposes he made you for. It's really the only way to live. Everything else is just existing. Real life begins by committing yourself completely to Jesus Christ. If you are not sure you have done this, all you need to do is receive and believe. The Bible promises, 'To all who received him, to those who believed in his name, he gave the right to become children of God.' Will you accept God's offer? First, believe. Believe God loves you and made you for his purposes. Believe you're not an accident. Believe you were made to last forever. Believe God has chosen you to have a relationship with Jesus, who died on the cross for you. Believe that no matter what you've done, God wants to forgive you. Second, receive. Receive Jesus into your life as your Lord and Savior. Receive his forgiveness for your sins. Receive his Spirit, who will give you the power to fulfill your life purpose. The Bible says, 'Whoever accepts and trusts the Son gets in on everything, life complete and

forever!' Wherever you are reading this, I invite you to bow your head and quietly whisper the prayer that will change your eternity: 'Jesus, I believe in you and I receive you.' Go ahead." (Warren, 61)

Danny closed the book and reflected. He had so many doubts still. He really liked what he'd been hearing about God and His nature, heaven and forgiveness and all that stuff, but this Jesus thing was still a stumbling block. *Can I follow God and not fully believe in Jesus?* he questioned. He remembered one of Tammy's admonitions. "Most people say show me and then I'll believe. God says, believe and then I'll show you." So Danny, on that sunny Sunday morning, closed his eyes and thought, *God, I believe in you and I receive you. I ask you to help me better understand what all this means.* It was the first prayer he'd conjured since he was twelve years old.

He closed the book and looked over at Julie, who was driving. "Well, you're probably going to be a bit shocked, but I just told God I believe in Him and receive Him."

"Seriously! That's great! What made you decide to do that?"

"I've been getting to like this Jesus character, and Rick Warren just invited me here to say it, so…" Danny just shrugged his shoulders and trailed off. But it really wasn't a little thing to him. He felt some kind of satisfaction and pride in his choice. At church, he and Julie eagerly told Jer and Tam, then Pastor Jones. Their beaming faces reflected Danny's inner self. Christians love it when a prodigal child seems to find his way home.

But those pesky doubts lingered. And they were legion. *Everyone seems to buy in to evolution, and it makes sense. How can the Bible be compatible with that? The Bible seems fanciful and made up. How can I trust it if it's just made-up stories? Why doesn't God just show himself to people? He could make it so much easier for us. How can I trust the*

Bible when some of the rules it commands seem so out of step with my conscience?

As much as Danny's life was finally getting on the right track, it was only one step in that direction. Like the seed that's planted on a rocky path, he was vulnerable to withering. And you know Satan, who had long ago dispatched and moved on from Danny, was suddenly taking a renewed interest in him.

Chapter Sixteen

THE TRAP

2003

James 1:13-15 – God cannot be tempted by evil, nor does he tempt anyone; but each person is tempted when they are dragged away by their own evil desire and enticed. Then, after desire has conceived, it gives birth to sin; and sin, when it is full-grown, gives birth to death.

A few weeks after Danny made his confession and started interacting with God once again, he found himself in a Towncar with a couple of executives from his company, headed to the airport on their way to Seattle for a big meeting with Boeing. In his briefcase was *The Purpose Driven Life*, which he'd been eagerly reading each day per the schedule. He was so excited about the revelations he'd been learning, he was like a kid who just discovered candy for the first time. Anyone who'd listen, he'd tell them, "Heaven is a gift! You don't earn it by obeying rules. Isn't that great news?" It was like the world had become clearer somehow. Like he had been looking at things through a thick fog, and now the sun cleared the day. His purpose for living wasn't to make himself great anymore. His purpose was to know God and make Him great. *How could I have not been told this before? How could all of my family and friends and church services have not understood and told me about this?* Even on this drive, one of the executives brought up their church service the day before and Danny couldn't help but join in with enthusiasm and rave about the book. God was at work all around him, and he was finally able to recognize it and join in.

The meetings in Seattle were uneventful. There was plenty of downtime for Danny to read the short book chapters each day and to work on writing up his testimony. Pastor Jones had asked for people to relay how the book and series had impacted their lives, so Danny began eagerly penning his story. Who would have imagined the selfish, logical, militant agnostic would become the evangelist? He certainly didn't and neither did anyone who knew him.

Finding himself alone for the evening the last day of the trip was a pleasant surprise for Danny. Most trips involved dinners with employees or customers. To have a free night was normally a blessing; he could squeeze in a workout, grab a bite to eat, and relax. Only being alone this night is exactly what Satan hoped for.

She sat down next to Danny as he ordered his dinner at the bar. It was a higher-end lounge at the Hilton with dim lighting and shelves lined with illuminated bottles of top-end spirits. Danny looked over and gave her smile and a nod. She was an average-looking girl, maybe a few years younger than him, nothing to make him look twice. The lounge was mostly empty and quiet, save for some light piano music playing in the background. Danny finished his beer and pushed it toward the rail to signal a refill, and as his glass was being tended to, she ordered herself a dry martini.

"You really like those?" Danny asked, breaking the awkward quiet.

"Oh yeah," she replied, looking him deep in the eyes, "this is my drink. You must have never had one made right."

"Maybe? I'll admit, I tend to stick with beer."

"You have to use Gray Goose. And three olives."

The conversation flowed effortlessly. For Danny, two beers turned into four. For her, one martini turned into three. It was all very benign, friendly, innocent. But then it wasn't.

"Danny," she said, turning toward him and resting her hand on his bare forearm, "I have a bottle of wine up in my room. Why don't we save a few bucks and move this party up there?"

Danny hesitated for a second. But unfortunately, the hesitation was just long enough for Danny's ego creep in and nothing else.

She headed to her room on the eighteenth floor, and Danny stayed back to pay his bill. His palms started to sweat. *I'm just going up for a drink*, he tried to assure himself. *No big deal.* He knew it was a lie, but the chase took control. He signed the receipt and headed for the elevator.

Pressing the button for the eighteenth floor, Danny noticed his hand was trembling. He made a fist then opened and closed his hands a couple of times. As it started going up, he quickly pressed twenty-one. *I'm not going*, he thought. *Just go to bed.*

He felt his weight lighten and watched as the doors slid open at eighteen. On autopilot, he stepped off and the doors closed behind him. The empty elevator headed to his floor without him. Spinning with intoxication, he squinted to read the placard with the room number directions and headed to the right.

The long narrow hallway stretched before him. It seemed he had a mile to go, but he trudged along like his feet were wet with mud. His whole being swirled with anticipation, fear, regret and his breathing was heavy, like he was readying to rob a bank.

He got to room 1833 and stood outside the door, staring. "This is not a good idea, Danny," he exhorted under breath. "Just go back down to the bar and have another drink there. Nothing good can come of this." His heartbeat was almost audible.

Voices peppered his mind:

It's no big deal.

You know you want this.

Just do it.

Be a man.

Why are you here?

Is this who you are?

You should go.

ARE YOU DONE YET?

The last voice made Danny look to his left as if he expected someone to be standing right there. In a panic, he took off full speed down the hall. He ran right past the elevator and leapt up the three flights of stairs, emerging on his floor. He approached his room and fumbled for his key card. He inserted it into the slot. Red flashing light. He tried again. He looked around, making sure he was at the right room. He desperately wanted in. He wanted to be locked in. Safe.

Slowing down, he finally got the door unlocked. He burst through and turned, forcing the door shut and latching the deadbolt. Standing there short of breath, he noticed his reflection in his peripheral vision. He turned and got within inches of the glass. The entryway light cast an ugly shadow on his baggy eyes and lit up the red bloodshot therein. "What the hell was that?" He yelled. His deep breaths fogged a small circle in the mirror. "Seriously? Is this who you are? Is this who you want to be?" Danny's face turned from shock to anger, and he slapped it as hard as he could. "You can't go down this road with God and do this kind of s#it! No More!"

Danny's breathing slowed and he purposefully took some deep breaths, stepping back from the mirror. He closed his eyes. "God, please take this temptation from me. Keep it away from me. Protect me, Lord. Protect my heart. Protect me, please."

Danny laid down on his bed, fully dressed, and he kicked off his shoes. *No more flirting*, he ordered himself. *You can't tell people how great God is and do that stuff, you hypocrite!*

He almost ruined everything. But God had a hold on Danny and wasn't letting go so easily. This was a big step, but still had his doubts. One in particular which would make him susceptible to relapse. One doubt that would keep him from fully walking this road that God would have him on. One insurmountable doubt that would keep him from God's peace, His purpose, and from His presence.

Chapter Seventeen

THE WAR WITHIN

2004

Mark 9:24 – Lord, I believe; help me with my unbelief!

It was the fastest flight to Connecticut he ever had. Danny stood up to get off the plane, and he put the book in his briefcase.

"You like that book?" the stocky guy across the aisle asked in a thick Northeastern accent.

Danny was a little surprised. "Love it," he admitted with animation.

The guy nodded, "Yeah, I read it a few years ago."

"You like it?" Danny assumed.

"Nah, not really," he said shrugging his shoulders and departing the plane ahead of Danny.

How could he not like this book? He wondered. Danny hadn't been able to put it down, save to sleep for six hours the night before. He was a hundred and fifty pages in and couldn't wait to pick it back up. But first, get to headquarters, do his job, and have dinner with his boss. The book would have to wait.

Ever since that sunny Sunday four months prior when Danny took his leap of faith, he'd been having an internal debate—a war of sorts between his inner Mr. Spock and his newfound Spirit. Growing up, Danny learned to "control" his emotions, or more aptly, hide them. His mentor for this was a character from his favorite TV show, "Star Trek." The emotionless, highly logical alien with pointy ears was the perfect muse to emulate. And he had become so much a part of Danny's persona that he couldn't help but point out the newfound inconsistencies in his beliefs. Those inconsistencies created an unrest which Danny couldn't quell.

So with the intensity of a madman, he tore into those doubts. He read everything he could get his hands on and talked with friends and pastors alike. He studied the history of the Bible. He read books like *About Grace* and *Mere Christianity*. He even read the Bible itself. As doubts were assuaged, sometimes new ones emerged. But each encounter created a debate pitting the Holy Spirit against Mr. Spock.

"Maybe Christ was just a great man and teacher, and his influence was so moving his followers eventually began to inflate his teachings with miracles and legends?" Mr. Spock questioned.

So Danny read about the Gospels—the books of Matthew, Mark, Luke and John—who wrote them; when they were penned; how long it takes legend to creep into ancient writings.

"See," the Holy Spirit would retort, "I moved those men to write what they saw. You have accurate recordings of what happened. And if you don't trust me yet, remember what C.S Lewis said about Christ:

> 'I am trying here to prevent anyone saying the really foolish thing that people often say about Him: I'm ready to accept Jesus as a great moral teacher, but I don't accept his claim to be God. That is the one thing we must not say. A man who was merely a man and said the sort of things Jesus said would not be a great moral teacher. He would either be a lunatic — on the level with

the man who says he is a poached egg — or else he would be the Devil of Hell. You must make your choice. Either this man was, and is, the Son of God, or else a madman or something worse. You can shut him up for a fool, you can spit at him and kill him as a demon, or you can fall at his feet and call him Lord and God, but let us not come with any patronizing nonsense about his being a great human teacher. He has not left that open to us. He did not intend to.'" (Lewis, 53)

"I see," Mr. Spock would admit. "But since there are contradictions within the Scriptures, it is logical to assume they were written by men with differing agendas. How can something from God have errors in it?"

"What inconsistencies, Danny? Find them and show them to me."

So Danny looked up Bible contradictions: Is the creation story the same in Genesis 1 and Genesis 2? Where were the Ten Commandments given, on Mount Sinai or Mount Horeb? Does Paul teach salvation by faith while James teaches salvation by works? There are hundreds of "contradictions" or questions buried within the Bible that people have documented over the course of time. And with each one that Danny researched, he also found reasonable answers for the differences.

For example, John 3:13 says: "No one has ever gone into heaven except the one who came from heaven—the Son of Man." But 2 Kings 2 reports that Elijah had ascended to heaven. How can Christ say no one has gone into heaven when 2 Kings 2 reports the opposite? The resolution to this resides in the context of what Christ is saying in John 3. He is saying He has come to teach about heavenly things. And no one on earth had been in heaven to have the first-hand experience by which to teach these things, except for Him. So the contradiction only exists when you take the words out of context and are ignorant about what's really being conveyed.

"So you see, Danny," the Holy Spirit comforted him, "the reason why I allow these apparent problems to exist is to deepen your faith. I am more than what can be defined in writing. I want you to use Scripture to help bring you closer to me, not as a book of rules to replace me."

"But even if the Bible is accurate and true," Mr. Spock interjected, "it's equally likely the other world religions are also accurate and true, just from a different perspective. It's like explaining an elephant, where one book describes his trunk and another his ears, yet another his hooves."

"But I precluded that possibility when I proclaimed that I am the way, the truth, the life, and no one comes to the Father except through me. There's no logical way to reconcile my statement with the statement that the Koran is God's final revelation or that the Bhagavad Gita is another way to me. And if you're going to logically evaluate which of the so-called holy books to believe, you'd sure do well to pick the one written soonest after the actual events, has more manuscript copies from ancient times, and is corroborated by multiple accounts, including accounts outside the Bible."

One by one, Mr. Spock raised an objection, and one by one, the Holy Spirit led Danny to the real logic, the real truth. But in the back of his mind, there was this one lingering doubt. Danny was sure it was an irrefutable doubt. One that would forever haunt him and keep him from fully trusting in Christ. He was barreling headlong toward this doubt, and he knew it. And as its presence in his mind grew larger and larger and seemed just about to cool his warming faith, that's when he was introduced to the book he was so eager to continue reading.

A Case for Christ is a recounting by author Lee Strobel about his journey to faith. As a committed atheist and an investigative journalist, Strobel had been on the same road as Danny many years prior. And like Danny, he harbored many of the same doubts.

Upon seeing the premise, Danny tore eagerly into the book. Piece by piece, Strobel interviewed renowned experts and put together the underlying argument: You can trust the Bible about Jesus.

Were the Gospels written by credible eyewitnesses? Yes, they were. Were those accounts reliably preserved over time? Yes, they were. Did Jesus actually believe he was the Son of God? You better believe He did. Strobel's PhD experts enumerated evidences and rationale sufficiently convincing Mr. Spock on doubt after doubt. And after each argument, Mr. Spock would whisper mockingly: "But they could have just made it all up."

They could have just made it all up. That was the one doubt Danny knew couldn't be overcome. Did Jesus fulfill all the prophecies about the Messiah the Old Testament predicted? Sure. But the Disciples could have just made it all up. They could have been so moved by the man Jesus and so driven by power or altruism or whatever that they made it look like Jesus was the Messiah.

Was Jesus's death a hoax? Doesn't look like it. After all, they report putting a spear in his side with blood spewing out. But what if they just made that up? That's still a plausible explanation.

Was His resurrection just a mass hallucination? Nope. Mass hallucinations don't happen. Maybe it was a twin? But what about the holes in the hands and in his side? Not likely to be a twin either. But maybe they just made it up?

The body was missing from the tomb, but maybe the disciples just stole the body? Not likely as it was guarded by Romans who would have been executed for allowing such a thing to happen. But what if the Romans weren't there? What if they took the body and just made up the resurrection? It could have happened. And it seems more plausible than a resurrection, doesn't it?

Every time an argument was demolished, Mr. Spock would raise the possibility, no, the probability, that the best explanation for the Jesus narrative was that it was invented by the disciples. And Danny had to nod his head in agreement.

So sitting down in his window seat on his return trip from Connecticut, his excitement about the book was starting to wear off. He was starting to feel defeated, tired. All this debate, all this research and what would it prove? The Bible says you can't please God without faith. Maybe this was his point. Everyone has some point where they can't explain something. *Maybe this is my point? Is it even worth reading anymore?*

Danny looked out to the light snow beginning to fall, and the captain came on to let everyone know they'd be delayed for de-icing. He stared down between his feet at the briefcase and rubbed his eyes. He grabbed the Hemispheres magazine from the seat-back pocket and thumbed through it. The crossword puzzle was already filled in. *Who cares about three perfect days in Bali?* With nothing more intriguing, he grabbed the book and filled the time.

The plane eventually accelerated down the runway. Danny closed his eyes and enjoyed the feeling. If only his inner turbulence could be more like the lilting kind one experiences during takeoff. But his inner turbulence wasn't the gentle at all. It was frantic, stomach-churning. It felt more like a crash.

He resumed reading. Eventually he reached the final chapter: "The Circumstantial Evidence." An interview with Dr. J.P. Moreland. *Circumstantial evidence*, he thought mockingly, *I guess we're done*.

But as Danny turned the page, he saw an intriguing subtitle. Exhibit 1: The Disciples Died for their Beliefs. His attention became rapt, and the busy world of the airplane attendants faded out of consciousness as Moreland described how the disciples had nothing to gain by claiming a resurrected Christ and everything to lose. They would live lives of persecution and poverty, and most of them would die for their claims. He read as Strobel initially made Mr. Spock's argument for him:

I interrupted with a "Yes, but…" objection. "Yes," I agreed, "they were willing to die for their beliefs. But," I added, "so have Muslims and Mormons and followers of Jim Jones and David Koresh. This may show that they were fanatical, but let's face it: It doesn't prove that what they believed was true."

"Wait a minute—think carefully about the difference," Moreland insisted as he swiveled to face me head-on, planting both of his feet firmly on the floor.

"Muslims might be willing to die for their belief that Allah revealed himself to Muhammad, but this revelation was not done in publicly observable way. So they could be wrong about it. They may sincerely think it's true, but they can't know for a fact, because they didn't witness it themselves."

"However, the apostles were willing to die for something they had seen with their own eyes and touched with their own hands. They were in a unique position not to just believe Jesus rose from the dead but to know for sure." (Strobel, 268)

Danny's eyes widened at first and his breath was shallow, his lungs full of air. He read the passage again. *Is this the answer?* He raced to find Mr. Spock to ask him, but he wasn't there. *Oh my God*, he realized. *That's it!* He exhaled and started breathing again and closed his eyes, sandwiching the book around his index finger in his left hand. For the first time in a long time, the voices in his head were quiet. The turbulence was gone.

"I'm so sorry," he mouthed to himself over and over. "I was wrong. I'm so sorry."

With new eyes, he opened his and looked around the cabin. It's like he could see right through people. Their lives seemed so pointless. Typing away at emails, serving drinks, reading magazines. *I wonder if they know? I wonder if they care?* The gentle hum of the engine underscored the serenity of his mood.

People don't die for something they know is a lie, he knew. *They might die for a cause or for love, but not for a lie. And certainly not dozens or hundreds of people. If the disciples made up the story, there's no way they'd go willingly to their deaths. But if they actually saw what they claimed they saw, there's no way they wouldn't. It makes complete sense.* Danny's cheeks widened as a sated smile came to his lips. *I can't wait to share this with everyone.*

When he got home that evening, he excitedly told Julie about what he'd read. She reflected his enthusiasm. From that point, their walk with God shifted from low to high. They were soon baptized, and Danny got to share his testimony with the church. Their marriage became healthy, loving and respectful. They started serving in various ways, at the church and in the community. They learned to be more generous with their money and possessions—reflecting their gratitude for all they'd been given. Danny and the family experienced the promises of the Bible firsthand—love, joy, hope and purpose.

But God is always on the move. There's always another step. There's always something new. In the midst of Danny's tranquility, the Holy Spirit began to whisper again.

"You're telling everyone about me, but what about your father? What about your father?"

Chapter Eighteen

REUNITED

2005

Hebrews 13:3 – Remember those in prison as if you were together with them in prison, and those who are mistreated as if you yourselves were suffering.

Danny walked into the sprawling lunchroom and eagerly looked around for signs of life. If he hadn't just walked through the airlock-like double-doors of security he would have sworn this was a high-school cafeteria. The lights were all off, save for a few along the walls. The windows at the opposite end revealed the sunlit palm trees of Florida, their shadows reflecting off the glossy tile flooring. Some tables were out with their integral round seats, but many others were folded and lined up against the longer wall.

Danny was surprised and disappointed his dad wasn't already there waiting for him. After circling the room once, he took a seat on the table top and faced Dave's most likely entry point, a beige steel door with a tiny head-sized rectangular window.

For the first time in a decade, he was about to see his daddy. How much had changed since then: graduated college, got married, three kids, two new homes, in management for a large company. Oh, and that whole Jesus thing.

God had been orchestrating this visit for months. Shortly after his baptism, Danny started mailing letters to his dad describing his experiences. "It amazes me that I went to church services, had conversations with people, and no one ever told me about all of this," he wrote. "I can only assume they don't understand it themselves or they'd surely want to talk about it. How about you? Is this 'news' to you?" Unfortunately, his dad was fairly unresponsive, seemingly unimpressed. Danny tried bringing it up on their bi-weekly phone calls, too, but his dad didn't grab the bait when he'd throw out the line. So God finally encouraged: *Go see him; it's been too long*! And as God is known to do, He arranged it so Danny didn't have any excuse not to. A business trip to south Florida conveniently arose so he was able piggy-back on that and drive up from Miami.

Danny had to get special permission for this rendezvous as the timing of his trip wasn't going to coincide with normal weekend visitation hours. That suited him just fine. Not only would it avoid the awkward frustrations of shuffling through the waiting rooms and security with a bunch of strangers, all there because their families or friends were social deviants, but it would also be a calmer, less distracting environment.

Danny reminisced on the two-hour drive from Miami about the scores of visits he'd made over the years. His earliest memory was shortly after his tenth birthday, prior to any convictions. It was more like a visit to an office building except for the jumpsuit his dad was wearing. So naive back then, they all figured he'd be home in months. From there it moved to the more typical environments of bars, cuffs, and bullet-proof glass. To be fair, most of the places had some sort of courtyard or visiting area that was less intimidating than the real life the prisoners endured. A pleasant façade to prevent the familial angst. Danny used to look forward to those visits: playing blackjack, eating candy bars from the commissary, and sipping on sodas. The worries and bustle of life faded away, and he could just be. From the early days in Florida until the auto parts businesses started struggling and closing, Danny had seen a half-dozen different prisons before he was sixteen years old. Reminiscing really brought things into perspective. He really missed being a kid. He really missed his daddy.

As he waited, he lightly drummed on his legs and actively looked around, trying to avoid surprise in case he was facing the wrong way. The nervous energy wasn't all due to anticipation; he was standing in a prison after all. Then finally, a sign. A head appeared in the tiny window in the door. From the egg shape and lack of hair, he instantly knew. He smiled. Dave returned it with a giant toothless grin. If Danny hadn't been so excited for this moment, his face would have morphed from joy to shock. He looked so much older. So less healthy.

The door buzzed and opened. Danny purposefully slowed his walk to meet him halfway. "Hello Daddy," he said as they embraced with a hug. It's like their bodies were made to unite like this, comfortable, familiar. Even the smell—Old Spice and cigarettes. When you're in the midst of them, you seldom realize the moments in your life you would want to relive over and over. Even as Danny's emotions connected this moment to hugs from his past, he knew this would forever be one of those moments. Oh, for time to stand still.

"Let me look at you," Dave said, looking through his glasses as they ended their embrace. Their eyes scanned each other. In the ten years, Danny hadn't changed so much; he was still lean and muscular, maybe his forehead slightly taller. Dave had always been softer physically, but now thinner and somewhat gaunt. Danny tried not to stare at the hole where the top front teeth should have been in his daddy's smile.

"How was the drive up from Miami?" he asked, trying to make the scene comfortable.

"Easy, about two hours," Danny replied through his grin. "Is this where you eat, I assume?"

"Three squares a day. The food here ain't too bad, especially compared to Homestead. On holidays we even get turkey dinner with mashed potatoes." Dave's voice sounded different. The missing teeth made sounding out words like "teeth" difficult. As happy as Danny was to see him, it was also beginning to break his heart.

They slowly walked around the room while they caught up. Danny bragged about his kids and his job. Dave mostly complained about the inmates who caused him grief. Nothing too serious, mostly mannerisms and bad habits that got on his nerves. And the inept medical care. "This doctor must have got his degree in Ecuador or somewhere. He doesn't know his @ss from a hole in the ground," he lamented.

They paused by the vending machines for a minute; Dave looked over his old glasses up and down the selection. "What's that? That looks new." It was a Hershey bar with M&Ms. "I've never seen that one before," he said, his eyes lighting up. He turned and looked in Danny's eyes. "Can you buy me one of those?" he asked. You would have thought Dave was five years old, asking *his* daddy for a treat. It dawned on Danny how much his life had changed. Suddenly, roles were reversed. As happy as he was to provide his daddy this simple treat, he realized just how pitiable his existence had become. And, as they caught up over the next two hours, how meaningless and purposeless as well.

They chatted a bit about the arrest and about Dave's "operation", but Danny didn't scratch too hard. Part of him didn't really care. He was just happy to be there and to be reunited. The time melted away like ice cream in the sunshine and before they knew it, it was time to say goodbye. Danny realized he didn't even get a chance to talk about his church or about God like he intended to.

"Dad, before I leave, can I pray with you?"

Dave's face went blank. He didn't say anything; he just did a quick double nod.

Danny closed his eyes and bowed his head. "Father, I want to thank you for enabling me to be here to see my dad today. Ten years was ridiculously long; please don't keep me away so long again. I ask for you to bless my dad in this place. Allow him some mercy from the trials and pains he endures. Help him get the medical care for his heart that he needs. But most of all, reveal your presence to him as he goes throughout his days. Bring some light and joy to his life. It's in Jesus's name I pray. Amen."

Danny raised his head and opened his eyes, seeing Dave remove his hand from under his glasses.

"Thanks, buddy," he said as they enjoyed a goodbye hug. Emerging from the embrace, Dave pecked Danny on the side of his lips, something he hadn't done since he could remember. They said their goodbyes and Danny departed.

The drive back to the hotel was painful. Danny called Julie to relay his experience. "You wouldn't believe how pathetic and purposeless his life is, Julie. It's so sad. I can't believe he's endured this for over twenty years."

As the miles passed by, the music from the radio combined with and amplified his emotions. As broken as he was over his dad's life, he also felt the ping of regret. *I missed a perfect opportunity after the prayer. Why didn't I just ask him to accept Christ right there?* Regardless of whether Dave would have responded to Danny's invitation or not, or whether that response would have even been genuine, Danny felt like he missed a key moment. So he agreed with God that he would step up his game and water the seed he believed he just planted.

And cultivate the soil he did. As quickly as they could reply to each other and wait for the postman, they began writing letters. Danny tried to make his evangelistic efforts seem natural, not forced. He'd weave them into his dissertations about how life was going, as if Jesus was just another family member doing cool things, helping them out. As the letters progressed, Danny became more overt with his intentions. In one letter he wrote:

> You know what's more amazing than knowing I'm good to go to heaven when I die, it's that God really provided meaning and purpose to my existence. I struggled for years to create some significance. I remember telling Julie that I'm going to be the best boss somebody ever had. And while I still harbor that desire, it's totally secondary to my real purpose for being alive. I have the most significant job to do that anybody could ever have. I get to work with God to bring heaven here to earth. To help bring people into a relationship with Him and be a light to the darkness. I know this probably sounds weird coming from me, like I'm part of a cult or something. But it's all right there in the Bible. Incredible that I never knew all those years.

Through all of Danny's efforts, spanning years, Dave never really got it. "Religion just ain't for me," he'd say.

"Religion ain't for me either, Dad. It ain't about religion; it's about a relationship." It didn't sink in. Danny even sent him some books hoping they'd help, including *The Purpose Driven Life*, which had been so pivotal in his own experience. But Danny's soil had been cultivated over many years—with music, relationships, life's lessons. Dave's had been hardened like clay. The seeds just couldn't sprout.

In late 2008, Dave's phone calls suddenly stopped. The family was rightly worried. Grandma Alice called everyone she could think of to find out what was going on. Not surprisingly, he suffered a heart attack which moved him into a medical facility. Before he could recover from that, an infection moved him to another facility. Then another. Alice was able to talk with him on rare occasions, but his condition didn't allow him to return to prison and his usual cadence of life.

As bad as the usual cadence was, this was worse for Dave: IV needles, uncomfortable beds, even worse food. But the worst of all, for the first time in his life, Dave felt truly helpless and alone.

Chapter Nineteen

THE CALL

Late August 2009

Mark 10:27 – Jesus looked at them and said, "With man this is impossible, but not with God; all things are possible with God."

He almost dropped his cell phone when she told him.

Several weeks had passed since he learned of his dad's death in that call at work from his Aunt Sandy, but this call rocked him in a completely different way. He almost fell into his chair in the den as Grandma Alice continued to explain.

This wasn't the first time they had talked since his dad's passing. Danny had gotten home from his jog that difficult day with his newfound peace in tow. He had explained to Julie about his run, about his prayer, that he was sad but satisfied. He made the tough call to his grandma, knowing it would be hitting her harder than anyone else. It couldn't be easy for her to outlive her child, even though he made it to sixty-three.

The call that day had gone as well as he could have expected. He purposefully hadn't gotten into it with her about the peace he felt on his run. Though Danny had frequently talked with Alice about God over the years, he wasn't exactly sure how comforting He would be for her now.

Had her interest been polite dialogue with no depth, or was it truly a meeting of the hearts? He had decided to just give her empathy and understanding. A shoulder to cry on.

She had been more stoic during that call than he expected. The decades of mourning had taken their toll already. Plus she had had a myriad of details to iron out. Would we get the body? When? What paperwork needed to be done? What about any insurance policies or Social Security? The busy work which occupies and distracts the ones left behind had already begun to consume her. As the call wound down, he offered up a prayer.

"Father, we thank you for our lives and for the life of my dad. We thank you, and we trust he is with you now, free of pain and suffering and hopefully playing a game of cards with Grandpa Whitey. Don't let them cause too much trouble up there until we join you. I pray you'll give Grandma clarity and a stress-free time now as she arranges for all that needs arranging. Make the answers to her questions clear and easy. Let us plan a gathering that honors You and allows us to remember him. In Jesus's name we pray. Amen."

Danny had teared up a bit after they hung up. His doubts about that card game with Grandpa Whitey lingered in his heart. Maybe they weren't enjoying themselves at all. He couldn't bear the notion. He went back to his mantra: *Trust God. I trust you, God. I trust you.*

Danny had gone to work the following day, and it was pretty much a day like any other, except that his mind wandered to his daddy more frequently than usual. As the days marched on, time did what it does and Danny started feeling less and less melancholy. He and his grandma would chat as she'd learn the details about something. He was to be cremated; the state would pay for that. They could get the ashes shipped to them. So on.

They had planned a gathering for early October. Alice wanted to spread his ashes by Whitey's grave. Sandy, Debbie, Mike, and their families would all be there. The whole family reunited once again. Danny and Dougie, too. Everything seemed to be falling in place, and life was getting back to normal. Then, there came this call.

"Hello Danny, can you talk right now?"

Alice's voice was livelier than normal; she sounded twenty years younger, and she had a sense of urgency to her tone telling him he better say yes. He wondered if Dave had a large insurance policy or something and maybe they'd be getting some money. But this was way better.

"You'll never believe what just happened," she started. "I got a call from that friend of your dad's, John, who's been writing to me for the past year while your dad has been shuffled to all those hospitals. He told me he got a phone call from another inmate who was in the hospital with your dad when he passed away. This inmate said that he wanted us to know that Dave wasn't alone when he died…"

That brought a smile to Danny's eyes. But before it could spread any further, she kept going.

"—and he said that your father accepted Jesus before he died, Danny."

He squeezed the phone to keep from dropping it and plopped awkwardly into the chair. "Whoa, what? Are you kidding me?" His tone was more skeptical than excited.

"No," she continued. "He said he was with your dad, and he accepted Jesus with him!"

"You gotta be kidding me!" But in his heart he knew. He was astounded. It immediately occurred to him: *You answered my prayer! You somehow went back in time and answered my prayer!*

But just to be sure, he asked, "This John guy, did he ask you for money or anything?"

"No, this other inmate said he promised your dad he would get ahold of me and tell us. Your dad told him that John would be able to."

"Wow," is all Danny could say. His heart raced like he was jogging. His emotions churned with gratitude, awe, joy, excitement. It felt to Danny like God had done the impossible, that He moved a mountain. He hadn't felt this kind of awe and gratitude since his plane ride home from Connecticut. It came over him like a wave. He raised his left hand, closed his eyes and worshipped as Alice continued.

"Can you believe it? John said he would write a letter and send along what few things he still had of your dad's. Some books and shoes and stuff I guess is all of what's left."

"Okay, this is great news, Grandma. The best. But sometimes these inmates are good con men. Make sure you don't give him money or anything like that." Danny's skeptical ways hadn't changed, even if his faith had.

"What money do I have to give? I'll forward the letter to you when I get it."

"Okay, Grandma. I still can't believe it. What an answer to prayer. Do you have John's address so I could write him? I'd like to thank him for everything." Which was only half true. He still wanted to feel out John and see if this was some kind of scam.

"Yeah, I'll have Sandy get it for you."

Thanks, Grandma, I love you."

"I love you too, Danny. Bye bye."

On September 24th, 2009, John replied to Danny's letter. Here's what it said:

"Dear Dan,

Thank you for taking time to write and express your deep feelings for your dad. To begin, I met you a couple of times when you and Doug visited at Dade, many years ago. Also, at all times, your dad keep me update with your schooling, your employment in Seattle and most exciting and proudful moments for him, the birth of each of his grandchildren. Even through those roughly ten years, your Dad never stop telling me how much he loved you and was, and is, proud of you. I have three grown kids (?), I should say a man and two women of my own, so I knew what he was feeling."

"I knew your Dad for about 26 years, 14 of those we were room partners and the rest we were in the same quad. The best friend I ever had, put up with and understood my strengths and weaknesses. No one understood how a Cuban from Miami and a northerner from Chicago could get along like brothers. I was the only one who could harp on him about his smoking and eating habits while, if someone else said anything, his sharp rhetoric would end his conversation. My family loves him, they know how good friends we were. When we were at different institutions for a couple of years, he would call my house every couple of weeks, so we would be updated on his health. A great human being and a great friend. Some guys here that knew him over the years still express what good person he was and how much he is missed. That is saying a lot of a person in this kind of environment. And it makes me proud to have been his friend."

"I have been a practicing Catholic all of my life, going to parochial school and graduating from LaSalle High School here in Miami. I even convinced your Dad to attend a couple of services back in the late 80s and early 90s but he never took it to heart. I brought him literature from the service, he would read it and give it back to me. That was even until just before he passed away. The inmate that was with him in the hospital told me that Dave accepted the Lord and was very much in Peace when he died. That kind of choked me up because I knew that eventually it would happen but hoped that it happened where he would enjoy living among us, so I could see the happiness in his face. I am glad, as I am sure he was, that you are living your life in the Lord here on earth. That is what I would have wanted for him too. My children are practicing Christian, my son and oldest daughter and their families attend a Baptist church. My youngest daughter ad my ex-wife attend Catholic services. I am very proud of them because they live a life of a relationship with the Lord."

"Like I told Alice, sometimes I get up and look toward his bunk whenever I hear a Cub score on the radio. I just can't believe his is not here. Your Dad was a great man and a great friend. He will always, as well as your family, be in my thoughts and prayers."

"Again, thank you for taking your time to write. May the Lord continue to give you guidance and protect you and your family."

"Sincerely, John Vicenti"

"PS: Give Alice and Sandy a big hug and kiss, I will write them soon."

Chapter Twenty

REVELATION

August 3rd, 2009

Revelation 4:8 – Holy, holy, holy is the Lord God Almighty, who was, and is, and is to come.

All he could hear was the monitor slowly sounding off, in sync with his struggling heart. His chest hurt, which wasn't unusual, and so did his arm as he tried to move it. The IV made his arm more purple than beige. The room was darker than typical for a hospital room. Dave strained to open his eyes. There was a dimmed spotlight above him, not aimed at his face, barely illuminating anything outside of his bed. The room was encased in white curtains, but it was much larger than usual. *This must be a special room*, he thought. The smell of iodine didn't mask the stench of death pervading the room. He'd smelled that stench many times before, and his heart monitor fluttered as it dawned upon him. He was alone. His eyes welled up.

How did I get here? He grimaced. *Am I still in Florida?* Fragments of memories swept through his mind, but just as he'd grasp onto one, it would fade into a blur with another taking its place: Ed McCabe. A masked doctor looking down at him in a bright teal room. Swimming in his pool, the cool water refreshing his skin. Chasing his boys up the stairs. Seeing that look on his mom's face when she heard the verdict—a look like she just buried her son. Falling down in a hard grey hallway.

His focus was disturbed by a faint rustling sound off to his left. He shifted his eyes as far as they would go, but he couldn't see what it was. He tried to will his neck muscles to turn his head, but it felt like it was nailed in place and his flesh would tear if he could actually move it. The beeping sound went faster for short while, then slowed to its previous pathetic pace.

Slowly coming into focus in his peripheral vision was a tall dark figure. "Dad?" he muttered. It seemed each step the man took in approaching Dave lasted for minutes. It couldn't be his dad, he reasoned; his dad passed away long ago. Maybe it was Danny? Did Danny come to…no. Was it his doctor?

Finally, he arrived. "It's not your dad, Dave; it's Gabriel."

Dave looked at this new thin face hovering over him with longish brown hair. He didn't know who this was. Still, he seemed familiar somehow, comfortable. He was relieved just to have someone there with him.

"You've been through so much, Dave. Do you know what's going to happen next?" he asked, his voice soft and soothing.

Dave knew, but he didn't. He hoped the man was going to do some procedure to save his life or something, but he figured that's not what he meant. No, he knew what he really meant. He slowly nodded his head.

"Are you afraid, Dave?"

The thought of being relieved of his pain was attractive, but his heart-rate monitor told a different story. *What a fool I've been*, he repeated in his mind. He had plenty of chances throughout the years, but now, now it was too late. Now he would have to trust his fate to God. Oh how he wanted to see his daddy again. How he wanted to hold his mommy. A tear dribbled down the side of his face as Gabriel gently wiped it dry.

"It's not too late, Dave. Do you trust me?" Gabriel's warm brown eyes stared deeply into Dave's. Dave paused for a moment, then nodded his head. "Do you trust Jesus Christ with the fate of your soul? Do you trust Him to stand before the Father on your behalf? To be your advocate?"

Dave's mind ran through all the supposed advocates he'd trusted over the years: Les Kipnis, Claude Kahn, Vic Africano, Brad Stark. None of them were able to save him. The other side always won. Satan won.

Almost as if he could read Dave's mind, Gabriel continued, "If Christ is for you, no one can stand against you, Dave. Do you accept Christ and trust Him alone for your eternity?"

Hypocrite! is what ran through Dave's mind. Deathbed confessions shouldn't count, he felt. *I ran my life the way I wanted. Why should I get forgiveness now that I'm helpless? Afraid. Desperate. I don't deserve it.*

"Nobody does," he heard someone else say. His eyes flitted around, but he didn't see anyone else. Gabriel just gazed upon him with a serious but warm smile in his eyes. Those words echoed in his mind: *Nobody does. Nobody does.*

He'd heard John say it over and over, but he never believed it. Danny believed it. Dave summoned some energy deep within his chest and drew in as deep a breath as he could. His chest welling with pain, he shouted out in a raspy whisper, "I do!"

Gabriel's smile moved from just his eyes to over his whole face, and he placed his hand gently on Dave's chest. The spotlight above his bed seemed to be getting brighter, and Gabriel started to look like a silhouette of himself. The spot where Gabriel rested his hand felt warm, and the heart rate monitor chirped with more and more urgency. Despite this, the warmth emanated from his chest and began to spread, to his neck, down to his belly, slowly pulsing out through his arms and legs until he was swaddled in it like a blanket.

Dave smiled, and his eyes closed. Somehow he could still see the light above his bed as if they were open. In fact, it was clearer now and even getting brighter. The sound of the monitor in his right ear was growing faster but fainter, and he could no longer feel Gabriel's hand, just the warmth. In the distance he could hear something quite faint. It was undiscernible, a white noise, but somehow also beautiful, like music or something. He wondered if his mind was playing tricks on him as the spot of light grew slowly larger and larger. Soon, the noise grew clearer and he could make out the singing.

"Holy, holy, holy," he heard. Was this really it? As the circle of light enveloped the whole of his vision, he started to make out faces, ghostly at first, white on white, barely discernible but not frightening. The singing now louder and clearer, "Holy, holy, holy."

Finally, he saw someone he knew. Danny! "How? How are you here?" Dave asked.

"I've always been here, Daddy," he answered.

Dave nodded his head, somehow understanding. They hugged, and Dave realized he was healed. He felt no pain, no weakness. And his whole body tingled with joy.

He looked around. His dad, his mom, sisters, brother, old friends and thousands upon thousands of people he had never met but somehow knew, all reached out with joyous welcome. In the center, a glorious, blinding throne. And Dave felt the beautiful song:

> "Holy, holy, holy,
> is the Lord God almighty,
> who was, and is, and is to come!"

And with a glowing smile, Dave faced the throne and joined the chorus.

"Thanks to King of Kings.

You are my everything,
and I do adore you!"

Amen.

AFTERWORD

Well, wow. What more can I say? God has indeed blessed me with a powerful testimony. And I hope it has blessed you too.

My dad wasn't an evil man. Surely he took part in some sinful activities and his discernment in picking friends is highly suspect. But he was just a flawed man, like me. A flawed man who went too far and suffered the consequences.

But make no mistake, the real tragedy in this story is not that my dad served his final twenty-seven years in prison and died there. It's that a man was murdered—Austin Dewey Gay. There are still competing theories about what exactly went down resulting in Mr. Gay's death. One view held it was completely unrelated to my dad's operation and Leonard Pease. It was just an unfortunate coincidence the prosecution used to nail the kingpin. Like using tax evasion to bust Al Capone. Another view was that my dad was completely in the know and ordered the killing. Obviously, the third view is the one I elected to put in the book. The evidence I've seen and the people I've talked to indicate that my dad did indeed run the organization, but that his control was tenuous; he was ignorant of the murder until sometime after it happened.

I don't know how Austin Gay's family was affected by his death. But I hope and pray God has used it to bring his family and friends closer to Him. I haven't thought about or prayed enough for them over the years. Please join me in starting to do so.

As mentioned, the parts of this story involving my dad and his "enterprise" were gleaned from various sources: court transcripts, depositions, newspaper articles, letters and interviews. Obviously I added quite a bit of my own "color" to those parts of this story. I made up conversations like the one in Chapter 2 between him and my Grandpa Whitey where he asked for money. But as always, this was done to communicate an underlying truth. My dad had an inferiority complex and yearned to show up his father. Grandpa was also competitive and stoked it. So hopefully the conversation just served to highlight that fact. I also made up the Survival chapter where my dad is in prison. My point there was to illuminate his life and that it was dangerous, but he was still in control.

An interesting aside on the whole lottery ticket scam of Chapter 13, I never knew why dad had me hold and resend lottery tickets for him. As I imagined back through it, the only explanation I could come up with was the messages-sent-in-code theory. I added the whole Gambino Boss wrinkle as he was indeed housed with one for a while. I imagined it more compelling than just him sending coded messages to whoever.

At any rate, if you're interested enough in the story to ask if any particular parts are true or embellishment and you don't already know how to contact me, feel free to send me an email at the address noted below. I'd be more than happy to elaborate.

Now, as for me, some parts of this story were difficult for me to relive and reveal: The whole being bullied and forced to sit in the mud. Being twelve and learning that my dad wouldn't be coming home anytime soon. Being a cheat. Of course that's the most embarrassing part. Even as recent as 2003, being tempted by some random woman at a hotel and almost succumbing. I still can't believe it myself. But, God has truly answered my prayer and taken away the temptation. He has protected me and my family. Julie questioned me about putting this stuff in the book, uncertain it needed to be revealed. But as inspiring as was my dad's conversion, this, for me, was more so. This is what God does—transform. I felt it important for you to see that in my life too. If it changes your opinion or perception of me, that's okay. Just as long as you realize that God's to credit for who I'm becoming today.

Before wrapping up, I feel I must comment a bit about the "bad influences" in the story, particularly my Uncle Mark. Mark was indeed a troubled soul and I was ripe for codependence. But I do feel this story only illustrates his more negative influences. At his core, he was a trustworthy friend who would do anything for those he loved. He was a teddy bear who had been hardened by the Marines, drugs and life's normal sufferings. He helped this insecure teenager gain confidence. In the end, he passed away from throat cancer in 2015. Before he died, I'm confident he got right with God. I am so glad to have called him both my Uncle and my friend, and I can't wait to see him (and Charley and Wayne) again.

Rich Kuduk is another who comes off as a bad influence, but at our ages, it was really just youthful mischief. I know our shenanigans crossed lines that most kids don't, but that wasn't Rich's fault. It was the confluence of unsupervised boredom and accessibility. A lesson learned that I brought to the raising of my kids. Rich truly was my bodyguard—just like the movie from 1980 of the same name. I used to think that movie was based on our lives, Rich even looked like the actor who played the bodyguard. But it was made before our travails. At any rate, I was grateful for his friendship back then despite the outcome.

Finally, my love and appreciation go out to everyone mentioned in this book, and beyond. I can't imagine my life here without your friendship and support.

For my wife, Julie: thank you for sharpening me and for not giving up when I made it very easy to do so. As we know, we're all a work in progress and I wouldn't be the man/husband/father I am today if not for you. I love you more.

For my mom, Linda: thank you for holding us all together in the middle of the hurricane you had to endure. I didn't realize all the turmoil you went through back then, and that in itself is a testament to your wisdom and strength. In the end, it worked out, and I couldn't be happier that you and Mike found each other.

For my surviving aunts and uncles: when a dad can't raise his son, it does take a village. You were that village. It's not lost on me how you took care of me and my brother. I'm sure you were just doing what was natural back then. You probably didn't consider it a big sacrifice or anything. But it was a big deal to us. Thanks so much.

For John Vincente and the other inmate (or Angel?) who made this story's ending so much better: to God be the glory! Right?

To God be the glory. Maybe that should have been my title?

All the best,

Dan "Danny" Domberg
ddomberg@gmail.com

Dave and his Sister Sandy with Danny and Tommy Brooks, meeting Jack Brickhouse at a Cubs Game. Circa 1978.

Mr. T visiting with Danny's family on July 4th, 1982 (Danny awkwardly shadowing everywhere he went)

Danny, Dave and Doug. 1995

LAKE CITY REPORTER FRI., FEB. 18, 1983

Kingpin?
Alleged drug ring boss tells very little

By JOE BLEWETT
Reporter Editor

Considered the central figure in a massive drug hauling operation which allegedly had as its off-shoot the 1978 slaying of Florida Agricultural Inspector Austin Gay, Robert David (Dave) Domberg Jr., 32, Palos Heights, Ill., is a close-mouthed man to say the least.

Charged along with five others in the conspiracy to murder former Agricultural Inspector Leonard Pease—believed by some authorities as a case of mistaken identity when Gay was killed—Domberg took the Fifth Amendment a total of 40 times when being cross-examined in a recent Madison County drug trial.

Domberg, who is being held in Columbia County Jail under a $1 million bond, is the operator of a chain of auto parts stores in the Chicago, Ill. area. However, authorities allege that his real operation was in drug hauling which extended from Miami to Chicago.

When cross-examined in the drug case on Feb. 11, 1983, by State Attorney Jerry Blair, Domberg repeatedly took the Fifth Amendment.

Excerpts from the cross-examination are:

Blair: Have you at anytime received any income from the sale or distribution of marijuana, cocaine or other illegal drugs?

Domberg: I take the Fifth Amendment.

Blair: Have you at anytime failed to report on your income taxes monies received from the sale or distribution of

(Turn to DOMBERG, P-2)

SUSPECT IN PEASE MURDER CONSPIRACY: Robert David Domberg Jr. (right) receives medicine from Columbia County Sheriff's Department medical officer Rodney Thomas. (Photo by Bill Graf)

SOURCES

Lewis, C.S. 1952. "Mere Christianity." New York, NY: Harper Collins.

Strobel, Lee. 1998. "The Case for Christ." Grand Rapids, MI: Zondervan.

Warren, Rick. 2002. "The Purpose Driven Life." Grand Rapids, MI: Zondervan.

Made in the USA
Middletown, DE
22 July 2019